Urban
Design
Review

A Guide for Planners

Hamid Shirvani

Planners Press
American Planning Association
Washington, D. C.   Chicago, Illinois

This book is dedicated to my parents.

TABLE OF CONTENTS

Acknowledgments

I wish to express my gratitude to Professor Robert Ponte for his guidance constantly and unstintingly given and to Professors Robert L. Geddes, Charles W. Harris, and Chester Rapkin for their invaluable help, advice, and encouragement. I am also indebted to many persons from public and private organizations for the time they generously spent in conversation with me. Included are the following: John Burg, Oliver Byrum, John Dobbie, Charles Gill, Roger Kipp, Weiming Lu, Lauren Otis, Richard Puffer, Stephen Quick, Jaquelin Robertson, John Sloan, and John West. The information they provided was of great help to me in gaining the necessary background. The views expressed as a result of these conversations are my interpretations.

Special thanks go to Professor Raniero Corbelletti, the Pennsylvania State University, for his unfailing support; to Nancy L. Daniels for her valuable editorial assistance; and to Susan E. Galistel, whose emotional support helped bring this book into being.

Hamid Shirvani
Newport Beach, California
October, 1981

Part I

Overview

Urban Design Review

1
Introduction

Urban design is a process "to safeguard environmental quality as a city changes."[1] It lies between the professions of city planning and architecture and deals with such issues as site selection and compatibility of a proposed building to its natural surroundings. Note, however, that in 1974 Robbins in an article about his work entitled "The Public Practice of Urban Design in a California Community" said, "I am practicing architecture in and for . . . the City of Fremont, California."[2] Is he equating large-scale architecture with urban design? Before full-scale war erupts among the professionals about who does urban design best, perhaps we could agree with Barnett. In speaking of "developing new professional skills to help shape urban growth and change," he says that there is a "national movement of architects and other professionals towards a greater degree of social involvement."[3]

Eckbo may have solved our dilemma: "Design is a process, not a person. . . . The quality of design is measured by the success of its solutions, once the wordscreen of salesmanship and promotion is withered away."[4] Too often, however, urban design receives insufficient attention.

A planner may show design sophistication in choosing an appropriate site for a building, and an architect may find that the most efficient and elegant design for the building is exactly suited to the context of the site. But what happens if the architect is forced to solve conflicts between the interests of the developer or investor, who is his client, and the needs of the community?

For example, a developer may plan an office building next to a small, historical park. The zoning laws permit an orientation of the building that turns out to be architecturally the most efficient. However, the building now completely blocks sunlight from the park at midday when members of the working community use the park. What should be sacrificed—the client's desires for an efficient building or the office workers' and citizens' lunchtime strolls? The situation is further complicated if the client is a private investor, dependent on conventional financing and perhaps less likely to yield to the community needs. The failure to consider, at the appropriate state of planning, the issue of urban design may result in misuse of resources which brings destruction of landscape and of old buildings and the construction of unimaginative box-like office towers, vast parking lots, and endless gridirons of low-income housing. However, is Lindbloom right when he says that the mere existence of a design review procedure is "often enough to eliminate ill-conceived design?"[5]

There has been both public outcry against failures in urban design and recognition of them by governments and investors. Acknowledgements of such failures, as well as the many successful examples of urban design, have increased demand for an organized and effective approach to urban design to link the political and departmental jurisdictions of a city or a region and assist in orchestrating "design decisions which flow from the separate jurisdictions."[6] Such a process is primarily concerned with "enabling of qualitative environmental change."[7] That is, urban designers lay the ground rules so that the architects, landscape architects, and engineers may design, build, and improve the quality of the physical environment. Michael and Susan Southworth's Lowell Discovery Network for the Model Cities Education Component of Lowell, Massachusetts is a perfect example of good urban design. In fact, it won them an AIA award for urban design. One of the judges, Archibald Rogers, explains why this design was outstanding:

> Each of our cities has its own kind of personality and what is recognized in this plan is the very particular personality which exists there. To pick out the essence of it as proposed here is a breakthrough in approach to urban design.[8]

The most commonly used and practical implementation tool for urban design is "design review." By design review I mean all the criteria and methods used in implementing urban design policies and/or plans, including both functional and aesthetic concerns. As an overall implementation tool, design review aids in regulating segments of the visual, sensory, and functionally built environment of a defined area in accordance with values and goals of the particular "community of interests" and relates design features such as pedestrian amenities and building massing to the sensory environment.[9] In other words, design review is the process of "evaluating property developments or development proposals to ensure that they meet a community's design policies."[10] The type of proposals that this process evaluates "may range from development of a site without buildings to construction, remodeling, or repainting, or even moving buildings onto a site."[11]

There are other meanings and interpretations for "design review." Let us consider, for example, what Lindbloom calls the need for "environmental design review." He states that despite "the usual development codes and ordinances and satisfactory levels of enforcement, . . . [there is] poor site planning, inadequate landscaping, signs that obscure adjoining signs, and buildings whose design completely ignores the design of neighboring structures and the surrounding environment." He also mentions the importance of well-drafted ordinances that do not "inhibit good design . . . or encourage mediocre design."[12]

Weismantel's discussion of design review calls it "legislating the urban design process" which he defines as "that decision-making procedure followed by architects and others professional designers in arranging structures, plant material, circulation and similar media on a site to meet perceptual criteria valued by expected users."[13] He then proposes a code to provide a legal framework to ensure that the professionals do indeed "follow" the procedure!

Contrariwise, Weaver and Babcock are quite emphatic: "We believe it is past hope that design will be left to the private market, and exactions as a condition of development permission are a way of life, increasingly sanctioned by the courts;" they further point out that it is more fruitful to inquire how to regulate the complexities of urban design.[14]

According to one report, design review is "esthetic control," a term which denotes "decoration" as well as the "psychological impacts of development on the ways people live and relate to each other, . . . every aspect of man's relationship to his environment."[15] The term "aesthetics" when coupled with "design review" may serve to perpetuate a false impression held by many persons that design review is solely concerned with beautification, architectural details, and style of architecture. Others make this distinction:

Aesthetics in connection with town planning concepts should serve
to improve the quality of the federal physical development with
special emphasis on the various types of urban attractions [to]
enrich the urban space and provide for not only sound business
interests, but also for human activity.[16]

This is a realistic definition of aesthetics as it relates to design
review.

In this book I use the term "design review" to refer to those
implementation processes that oversee and control public and
private development, ensuring that public amenities as well as the
general physical design of buildings are acceptable to the public. In
addition, certain residential neighborhoods may favor design
review to protect the distinct character of their areas. Thus, the
neighborhood may be designated a special district. Downtown
areas of the city may also want design controls for redevelopment
projects because "the public has a strong stake in the results."[17]
Moreover, historical areas, civic centers, and parks may be
designated special areas, too. Finally, such issues as sign control,
parking lots, landscaping, continuous retail frontage, and height
and bulk of buildings form a third category of control and usually
are part of the city's zoning ordinances.

While in general terms design review may apply to a variety of
aspects, in this book the term "urban design review" refers
specifically to the public aspects of design which encompass the
appearance of buildings and emphasize the effects of buildings on
their surroundings and on the city at large rather than considering
them individually.[18] To emphasize this point, let me say that design
review too often has been applied to individual projects rather
than the development of an overall policy.

Standards or guidelines used in urban design review differ
substantially from city to city and among jurisdictions within cities
depending on each body's urban design and planning policies.
While some cities have no standards or standards that are written
so vaguely that the urban design review process itself replaces
their use, other cities have very detailed standards which may be
written so precisely that specific "architectural styles, colors, and
materials"[19] are prescribed. In some instances, an urban design
agency may have the responsibility of establishing the standards,
or such an agency may merely provide a forum to create
rudimentary design review policies.

Urban design review should have built-in flexibility to judge each project on its own merits. Zoning regulations do not necessarily have the flexibility that urban design review has; generally, zoning regulations prohibit what are perceived as negative activities rather than encourage positive activities.[20] Master plans, too, may not be "sufficiently responsive to changing conditions to safeguard environmental quality. Advocates of review boards feel that they provide a mechanism . . . by which a community could exercise periodic judgements in response to specific development proposals."[21] But urban design review requires more than functional building and visually pleasing forms;[22] it should protect the interests of the public who are absent when the developers and their architects review their project.

Although the underlying purpose of design review to protect public interests is most clear when public resources or concessions are involved, the process may also be used to protect public property rights in more general areas. When development decisions have a potentially adverse effect on the public's perception of its spatial setting, a public regulatory body may undertake the task of reviewing those private decisions to protect the public good. After all, the developer often receives benefits and concessions from the public, and in return the public should obtain better urban design.

The following benefits may be derived from an urban design review process:

> Enhancing economic development opportunities; ensuring safe
> traffic flows; architectural harmony between buildings and
> landscaping; placing utilities underground; reducing signs and
> visual clutter; screening trash areas, junkyards or industrial sites;
> controlling glare, noise or odor from various uses; and
> coordinating historical preservation activities, including control of
> redevelopment within an historical district.[23]

An appropriately structured and administered design review process promotes better urban design for the public and provides a proper balance of the rights of the users and the developer.

The basis for public control of private projects is limited by the power of the state to enforce restrictions that mitigate adverse external effects of a development on its surroundings. The types of sanctions a city may use to enforce its controls depend on the sources of power and authority available to it. In the late 1960s, an

AIA Subcommittee on Design Review Boards recommended that such a board "be able to analyze the full reach of the law regarding design review."[24] The Committee on Design report includes a valuable discussion of the legal basis for design review which is beyond the proper scope of this book.[25] Lindbloom[26] and Weismantel[27] among others also suggest model ordinances for design review procedures.

Since 1978 HUD has specifically allowed funds to be used for UED (urban environmental design) in conjunction with CDBG (community development block grant) projects, though EIA (environmental impact assessments) had been required since 1969. The federal government further intended UED studies to encourage "citywide strategies" for "major public works and activities and major private investments" by technical assistance and by National Awards for Urban Environmental Design. HUD's Robert C. Embry saw effective local administration as the "key" to successful joint development. Optimistically, he said, "I foresee local government entering an era of conscious local urban environmental design administration."[28] Andrew F. Euston, Jr. of HUD listed the reasons for "this new need for local UED administration: citizen concern, costs, rising expectations, dwindling resources, lessons of the past, and complexity."[29]

Simultaneously with the new regulations allowing HUD funds to be used for UED, Landman was highly critical of HUD for its lack of guidance to local (often inexperienced) officials. She also charged that the required environmental impact assessment "focuses on inappropriate issues and poses inadequate questions." The result, Landman says, is that environmental quality is not protected and enhanced, and "impacts on urban design are largely ignored."[30]

She suggested that HUD train urban design reviewers (through mini-courses); provide a roving staff for on-the-spot advice to communities with CDBG grants; furnish "nontechnical environmental assessment guides;" encourage communities to develop community design guidelines; look for "substantive qualities in the work of local reviewers" so that there is "procedural accuracy, . . . specific discussion of impacts, . . . (and) evidence of public participation in the EIA process;" and "combine the annual performance report required by HUD with a cumulative environmental review."[31]

The manner by which cities initiate and administer urban design review programs varies among cities, depending upon implementation strategies. Specific situations may necessitate narrow, tightly-defined guidelines, while application of broad discretionary standards serves best in other cases. Other elements affecting the city's approach to urban design review include the overall objectives of such review, purposes for reviewing designs, internal organization and staffing, other actors immediately involved, and the absent future users.

Presently, various procedural models for the implementation of urban design are in use in U.S. cities. Some of these models might meet all common prerequisites for a productive urban design review process, but not all of them can work effectively under a full range of conditions. Thus, we need to examine the validity of a *particular* procedural model in a *particular* environment in which it is applied to meet the objectives of public and private concerns. Specifically, we might ask: What aspects of this model are suitable to this particular environment, and what are the crucial factors to be considered in making the process more effective in meeting the public's concerns?

In this book I investigate city government's implementation of urban design. My intention is 1) to examine the effectiveness of specific models of review procedures presently in practice, 2) to explore the relationship between model features and environmental considerations, and 3) to draw conclusions about the ways in which models can be applied in different environmental situations. I will analyze four generic model types and examine one application of each model, in an attempt to identify the specific aspects of urban design review that produce desirable or undesirable results and to explain whether or not the objectives were appropriate to a particular environment. After examining case studies of the models' application in four major cities, I shall make recommendations for valid models for design review in a variety of environments.

The book is divided into fourteen chapters. Following the Introduction, which provides a common base of understanding by presenting a brief overview of urban design review, I establish in Chapter 2 a framework for comparison of the models of design review I have chosen to study. I define the three basic components of all design reviews—approach, nature, and elements—and discuss the attributes and complexities of each component so that the reader will be able to identify them in the four models. Chapters 3–6 contain a careful analysis of the design review procedures in Boston (The Boston Redevelopment Authority), Minneapolis (Concept Plan Review), New York City (Fifth Avenue Special District), and San Francisco (Urban Design Review).

In Chapter 7 I use the framework established in Chapter 2 to thoroughly compare the models of design review and classify the components used in each city. I shall consider only the characteristics of the models themselves, leaving discussion of the environments in which they operate for analysis in the case studies, Chapters 9–12. However, I will discuss in Chapter 7 a fourth important aspect of design review, management—an aspect which strongly influences the success of the process.

Because the real test of any such ameliorative process is to determine how well it works when it is applied in the real world, Chapters 9–12 examine one representative case study in each of the four cities: Boston, Charlestown Savings Bank; Minneapolis, The Crossing; New York City, Olympic Tower; and San Francisco, One Market Plaza. The reader will see the interplay among the city government officials, profit-seeking developers, architects and designers concerned about their creativity being stifled, and the public whose interests must be served even though they usually are not present when design review takes place.

Do the procedures work as well as they are supposed to work? The book provides great detail in each case study so that the reader will have an intimate knowledge of the ins-and-outs of design review. Glimpses of the "actors" involved will provide the reader with a feel for the importance of the human element in design review. How important are personality, expertise, and willingness to "horse-trade"? Did design review provide each city and its public with a better product in each case?

Chapter 13, Findings, includes an extensive discussion of the environmental factors that influence design review procedures. Here we shall interject examples from other cities to illustrate further many of these factors. The chapter includes a list of 18 of the more important environmental factors a city must consider if it wishes to implement urban design.

Chapter 14 offers Recommendations which are presented in two different ways: 1) Based on the evidence in the case studies, how to make the approach, nature, elements, and management of design review more effective; and 2) How to choose a workable procedure in many differing environments. I offer practical guidelines to government officials and lay persons and to the professionals who assist them in the implementation of urban design. Students of city planning, urban design, landscape architecture, and architecture also will find this part of the book extremely useful in understanding the multiplicity of conditions that they may face when urban design is implemented.

Notes

1. Kevin Lynch and Donald Appleyard (1976). *Progress in Paradise?*, Vol. II (San Diego, Cal.: City of San Diego Urban Design Task Force), p. 27.

2. Jacob Robbins (1974). "The Public Practice of Urban Design in a California Community," *AIA Journal*, 62:25.

3. Jonathan Barnett (1970). "Urban Design as Part of the Governmental Process," *Architectural Record*, 147:131.

4. Garrett Eckbo (1963). "Urban Design—A Definition," *AIA Journal*, 40:37.

5. Carl G. Lindbloom (1970). *Environmental Design Review* (West Trenton, N.J.: Chandler Davis Publishing), p. 14.

6. Lynch and Appleyard (1976), p. 31.

7. Michael J. Pittas (1980). "Defining Urban Design," *Urban Design International*, 1:40.

8. "Lowell MA" (1973). *Progressive Architecture*, 14:104.

9. The term "sensory environment" (the "look, sound, smell, and feel of a place") is taken from Kevin Lynch (1976). *Managing the Sense of a Region* (Cambridge, Mass.: MIT Press).

10. Gerald R. Mylroie (1976). "Community Design Review Procedures," *Practicing Planner*, 6:25.

11. *Ibid.*

12. Lindbloom (1970), p. 4.

13. William Weismantel (1970). "Legislating the Urban Design Process," *Urban Law Annual*, St. Louis, MO: Washington University Law School, p. 196.

14. Clifford L. Weaver and Richard F. Babcock (1979). *City Zoning.* (Chicago: American Planning Association), p. 299.

15. American Institute of Architects (AIA) Committee on Design (1974). *Design Review Boards: A Handbook for Communities* (Washington: American Institute of Architects), p. 12.

16. F.A. Schwilgin (1974). *Town Planning Guidelines* (Ottawa: Department of Public Works), p. 12.

17. San Francisco Department of City Planning (1975). *Memorandum* to City Planning Commission from Dean L. Macris, Director of Planning, March 13, p. 5.

18. *Ibid.*, pp. 1–5.

19. *Ibid.*, p. 5.

20. Lindbloom (1970), pp. 14–15.

21. AIA Committee on Design (1974), p. 7.

22. Mylroie (1976), p. 25.

23. *Ibid.*

24. AIA Committee on Design (1974), p. 7.

25. *Ibid.*, pp. 12–31.

26. Lindbloom (1970), pp. 39–59.

27. Weismantel (1970), pp. 215–230.

28. Robert C. Embry (1978). "Urban Environmental Design Through Joint Development," *HUD Challenge*, 9:9–10.

29. Andrew F. Euston, Jr. (1978). "The Emergence of Urban Environmental Design," *HUD Challenge*, 9:2.

30. Wendy Landman (1978). "Environmental Impact Assessment and the Quality of Local Design," M.C.P. thesis, MIT, Cambridge, Mass., pp. 7–8.

31. *Ibid.*, pp. 92–100.

Part II

The Models

2

Design Review Models: A Framework for Comparison

This study will focus on four models for conducting design review so that we may cover the range of models most commonly used. In this book, "model" refers to a collection of procedures, processes, and guidelines used to conduct urban design review. I have selected four completely different settings in terms of geographic location, types of city administration, culture, homogeneity/ heterogeneity, high or low economic conditions, and so forth in order to give the broader perspective required for understanding and applying models of urban design review throughout the United States. These models and processes also represent a spectrum of the discretion used by the reviewers in conducting design review. We shall examine the Boston Redevelopment Authority's Design Review, The Concept Plan Review (Minneapolis), The Fifth Avenue Special District's Design Review (New York City), and the Urban Design Review (San Francisco).

The Boston Redevelopment Authority's design review model is intended to be applied city-wide, but its approach to specifying design requirements is much broader, leaving more discretion in the hands of the reviewer and offering less predictability for the developer and his architect. Minneapolis's Concept Plan Review is mandated for any residential development larger than ten units of dwelling. It is concerned with the compatibility of the proposed structure with the surroundings, based, with limited discretion, upon defined guidelines. New York's Fifth Avenue Special District is an incentive-type zoning program which attempts a balance of design issues and density related to the provision of site amenities.

San Francisco's Urban Design Review requires that significant developments be checked against the Urban Design Plan, thus providing considerable discretion based on the flexibility of the plan.

This chapter examines these models, delineates their common themes, and specifies aspects which differentiate the models. While each of the models analyzed here is embedded in the environment which generated its origins and influences its application, the emphasis of this section of the study is more on the characteristics of the procedures themselves than on the characteristics of their environments. I will discuss the environment's effects on procedures in Chapters 13 and 14.

Similarly, I will structure the comparative study of procedures for implementing design review around the purposes, organizations, and environments in which they are applied. I will analyze the three basic components of a design review process in this study—the approach, nature, and elements of design review—within a common framework which also will serve as the basis for matching design review models with various environments in Chapter 13.

First we must define in general terms the aspects of design review models, i.e., the approach, nature, and elements of design review, and we must also discuss possible attributes of each aspect. Then we will be ready to study each of the four models in detail.

Approach

The approach of design reviews may range from "self-administering" to "discretionary." Self-administering controls involve the use of detailed guidelines to explain the criteria that the review body will use to judge the proposed design, whereas discretionary controls give the power of interpretation and judgment to the reviewers. An example of a self-administering approach is The Zoning for Housing Quality, a resolution passed in New York City in 1975. The Housing Quality guidelines are stated in great detail—

terms are defined and information on application requirements and exterior and interior building requirements are provided along with a large number of illustrations which visually explain the regulations.[1] Thus, all information a builder needs to design an acceptable building is provided.

Descriptive labels are often attached to these two different approaches—"capital intensive" for the detailed self-administering approach and "labor intensive" for the discretionary interpretations.[2] The term capital intensive refers to the advanced planning and preparation of design guidelines that are necessary with the self-administering approach. With such a capital intensive approach, however, a comprehensive set of guidelines is prepared initially, and the design trade-offs or options are outlined. The developer and his architect then have the flexibility to select among the options. Thus, within a prescribed range, developers and their architects are given discretion to select the design trade-offs or options which are most appropriate for their projects. The options listed in the guidelines may be based on comprehensive studies or previous projects and may be updated periodically as new or improved design techniques are discovered.

The term labor intensive, however, refers to the efforts of the reviewers rather than the efforts of the developer and his architect. Often design reviewers conduct individual design studies and may possibly visit the project site to determine the guidelines to be applied. Thus, the discretionary approach may "tailor" the guidelines to each specific project; therefore, more time and effort on the part of the reviewers is required. Legislation and specific design review ordinances or regulations designate the amount of discretion design review board members may exercise.

Between these two opposite approaches to design review lie numerous other approaches. Between the self-administering, capital intensive approach and the discretionary, labor intensive approach are at least two incremental steps: 1) Self-administering—detailed guidelines automatically administered; 2) Semiself-administering—design review with narrowly interpreted guidelines; 3) Semidiscretionary—design review with broad guidelines interpreted and some limited discretion on behalf of the reviewers; and 4) Discretionary—design review without guidelines.

Another distinction of design review is whether or not the process itself is "formal" or "informal." Design review processes which are included in zoning ordinances or stated in specific design review legislation are called formal design reviews. In contrast, when legislation does not specify or mandate design reviews, the process is called "informal." Formal design review takes place because it is mandated by law, while informal design review takes place in the absence of legislation and is initiated by concerned governmental officials, interest groups, or the general public.

Nature

The "nature" of a design review model refers to the degree or level of detail provided in the design review guidelines. Two major dimensions characterize this nature: 1) Whether the guidelines are defined by "performance" or "prescriptive" standards, and 2) Whether the standards are accompanied by comprehensive prototypes or with references to specific design components. Performance standards are "based on public need, goals, and aspirations,"[3] and these standards state a criterion or quantifiable standard which a developer and his architect must meet. However, they have the option to select the method which will most effectively meet the stated requirement. For example, performance standards do not prohibit "any industry or use by name, but rather admit any use at all, provided that noise, vibration, smoke, odor, dust, fire hazards, . . . are under certain tolerable levels."[4] While the standard does not indicate the exact way to meet the requirements, it does specify a "test" which will be used to measure whether or not the developer and his architect have complied with the requirements. Santa Barbara's Design Review Manual contains the following example of a performance standard:

> Residential buildings not exceeding 3 dwelling units shall be provided with driveway access to within 150' of the most distant portion of any such structure. Driveway access shall have a width of not less than 16', overhead clearance of 13'6" and have a paved all weather driving surface capable of supporting a 32,000 pound fire truck.[5]

Prescriptive standards differ from performance standards in that they specify the characteristics of the final design but they do not require "tests" to assess the quality of the design element. The Fifth Avenue Special District guideline which requires that the ground floor of buildings be used for retail establishments is an example of a prescriptive standard.[6] Design review guidelines may be classified as either performance or prescriptive in nature or may contain elements of both.

The nature of design controls is also determined by the amount of detail included in the guidelines, the degree of discretion given the architect, and the types of examples which are used for illustrative purposes. The guidelines may state that designs are to look like "the building at Fifth and Sixth Streets" or on "State Street and Park Avenue." The main problem with using prototypes is the uncertainty which the designer may experience when trying to identify which aspects of the design are to be copied and where he/she is given the freedom to express his/her own creativity.[7] This situation is substantially reduced if slide analogues of accepted solutions are shown and the desirable elements identified for the designers.[8]

Design review guidelines may also focus on minute components of the design.[9] For instance, "all houses on State Street must have brown canopies" illustrates a prescriptive standard which emphasizes design components, whereas "all window openings must be large enough to admit an average of one percent sunlight into all interior spaces" describes a performance standard which focuses on a component of a design.

The nature of design review guidelines can best be thought of as a continuum. Whether the guidelines are performance- or prescriptive-oriented, emphasize individual components, or rely on prototypes depends on the characteristics of the elements being controlled as well as the degree of control desired.

Elements

The elements of design controls describe those aspects of a

proposed design—from compatibility of building structure with the surrounding area to details of architectural issues—which are controlled by design review guidelines. City zoning ordinance regulations may serve as the design review guidelines in some cases, or separate legislation may be passed to create the guidelines. In other cases there are no written guidelines; reviewers inform the developer and his architect verbally of criteria which must be included in their designs.

Elements can be divided into two aspects: 1) "Issues of concern," and 2) "Scope of issues." The former covers elements that are relevant to particular applications of design review, while the latter deals with the range of issues that the guidelines cover. "Issues of concern," then, refer to the elements that the guidelines are trying to control and may include particular design elements, architectural design, materials used, public amenities, and compatability of the new developments with the surrounding environment. In fact, design review guidelines are established in order to control or manipulate issues which are of concern to government officials and the general public.

Issues of concern may be separated into "functional" and "aesthetic" issues. Functional issues deal with the role of particular design elements, such as the use of arcades for shopping, circulation, and public amenity purposes, as well as sources of project impacts—traffic or pedestrian generators. For example, New York City's Greenwich Street Special District guidelines are concerned with functional aspects of design. One of the goals of this District is to develop a more efficient circulation pattern for pedestrians by connecting the buildings to each other and to the subways.[10] Thus, the issues of concern are functional since one of the goals of the Greenwich Street Special District is to improve the movement of people in the District.

Aesthetic issues deal with such architectural elements as color, texture, and level of detailing. The design review process contains for the city of Palm Springs an outstanding example of an aesthetic guideline: the standards state that building design, material, and colors are to be "sympathetic with desert surroundings" and that there should be a "harmony of materials, colors, and composition of those structures which are visible simultaneously."[11] The Design Review Manual for Santa Barbara contains similar aesthetic guidelines. In particular, the guidelines indicate that "skyline trees be incorporated into the landscape plan when practical" and that "building components such as windows, doors, and arches should have appropriate proportions to the structure."[12]

The scope of issues refers to the range or spectrum of elements covered under the design controls. The controls may focus on a few elements—height, FAR, coverage, and use—or be applied across the full spectrum of issues related to urban development. Thus, the scope of issues for which design review guidelines are developed may be unlimited provided that they are applied across the full spectrum of issues related to urban development.[13]

The distinction between the "nature" and the "elements" of design controls is that the nature refers to the level of detail incorporated in the guidelines, whereas the elements are concerned with the kinds of issues which are controlled and how they are related to other issues. While all of the previously mentioned elements may be controlled by design review, the intent of the guidelines and the degree of control or authority which the reviewing board or review ordinance has will influence the type of elements included in the guidelines.[14]

Notes

1. New York City Department of City Planning (1975). *Zoning for Housing Quality*, pp. 25–41.

2. Thomas Nally (1977). "Design Review, Alternative Models of Administration." Cambridge, Mass., MIT, unpublished M.Arch./MCP thesis, MIT, p. 215.

3. Weiming Lu (1977). "Successful Urban Design in Local Government," *Practicing Planner*, 7:33.

4. *Ibid.*

5. Santa Barbara Department of Community Development (1979). *Design Review Manual*, Section VI-B, "Fire Department."

6. *City of New York Zoning Ordinance* (1975). Special Fifth Avenue District, Chapter 7, Section 87–031, p. 145.

7. Nally (1977), pp. 217–218.

8. *Ibid.*, p. 218.

9. *Ibid.*

10. *City of New York Office of Lower Manhattan Development* (1971). Special

Greenwich Street Development District, and *City of New York Zoning Ordinance* (1975). Special Greenwich Street Development District, Chapter 7, Sections 86–00 through 86–13.

11. *City of Palm Springs Zoning Ordinance* (1970). Section 9403.00, p. 173C.

12. Santa Barbara *Department of Community Development (1979),* pp. 10, 12.

13. Gerald R. Mylroie (1976). "Community Design Review Procedures," *Practicing Planner,* 6:26.

14. Thomas Cooke (1976). "A Process for Community Design," *Practicing Planner,* 6:29.

3

Boston Redevelopment Authority Design Review

Like many cities in the United States during the 1950s and early 1960s, Boston was faced with deteriorating buildings and increasing numbers of people leaving the city.[1] Boston decided to launch an urban development program, financed in large part by the Federal government, to retain its "historic role as a center of commerce and culture."[2]

Strong political support for urban development was first expressed in the early 1960s when Mayor John F. Collins initiated the Boston Development Program to deal with the city's physical decline.[3] Mayor Kevin H. White, who was elected to office in the mid-1960s, continued to give support to urban development planning and design. State legislation created the Boston Redevelopment Authority (hereafter referred to as BRA) in 1957,[4] but the BRA did not become a productive instrument for urban redevelopment until Edward J. Logue, its director, combined planning and implementation into a single agency.[5] Combining the Planning Commission, Planning Department, and Urban Design function into one agency resulted in creating a strong centralized authority. The BRA incorporated "the rights derived from eminent domain, the prominence and prestige of key political and administrative figures, and the high priority they have given to design"[6] into an effective tool for urban design. Its objective has been to coordinate design activities in order to implement design objectives in Boston.

The BRA is involved with all urban development and redevelopment projects in Boston. The Urban Design Department of the BRA

guides the development of the physical environment of the city and the way it shapes how people deal with, perceive and respond to the city . . . helps formulate guidelines intended to direct the quality of the physical growth of the city that accompanies economic and social change—to balance this growth and change with the need to conserve Boston's special character, and to clarify the issues involved in making the urban environment more livable.[7]

The Urban Design Department conducts evaluations of design proposals and submits recommendations to the Authority. The Authority reviews all projects and is responsible for evaluating the quality and appropriateness of the proposed design to ensure that all of Boston's urban design policy objectives are met.[8]

The design review process conducted by the BRA has no written criteria or prescribed guidelines to follow, but members of the Urban Design Staff hold strong opinions about what constitutes good urban design. Their approach is incremental, focusing on small-scale government projects and individual private developments which will advance the cause of their urban design review objectives. The design review process affords them the opportunity to ensure that each case contributes desirable sensitivity and amenity to the urban environment.

The BRA does require the project's architect to prepare and present the following design plans at the review sessions: a Schematic Design, the Design Development, Preliminary Working Drawings and Outline Specifications, and the Final Working Drawings and Specification.[9] The Schematic Design includes a Site Plan, which emphasizes general relationships of the proposed building with existing buildings, and a Building Plan that explains the general architectural character of the building. The purpose of this review is to "secure agreement on and approval of the basic design concept prior to extensive work" by the developer's architect.[10]

After the BRA approves the Schematic Design, the architect then can submit the Design Development. During this stage of the review session, the architect submits plans of the final design so that they can be reviewed and approved by BRA prior to beginning detailed work on the preliminary working drawings. The third level of the design preparation requires the architect to submit Site Plan(s) and Building Plans that are developed sufficiently to describe "the character and scope of the proposal completely" and "all materials and assemblies comprising the building."[11] After the

Preliminary Working Drawings and Outline Specifications have been approved, the architect must submit completed site plans and working drawings. Construction of the project can begin only after the Final Working Drawings and Specifications are completed. The developer is strictly required to construct the project in accordance with the details of the approved drawings.[12] Thus, in Boston a building permit will only be issued after complete site plans and working drawings have been approved. This differs from the process in other cities where only the schematic and preliminary working drawings are discussed during the design review process. However, Boston's requirement does ensure that the completed project will not be different from the design which was approved in the design review process.

Despite the fact that Boston's legislation does not define or mention a formal design review process, all types of new developments must participate in Boston's informal design review process. Even though it is informal, it is definitely necessary and advantageous for both the developer and the city. For example, developers who want to build on private land must also go through design review sessions with the BRA unless they are willing to comply with very "restrictive" standards set by the city.[13] The "restrictive" standards were passed to ensure that all proposed development that takes place in urban Boston will be supervised by the BRA.

The BRA design review has a discretionary approach. The BRA urban design staff has the authority to evaluate the design quality and appropriateness of any proposed development in the city of Boston. Their function is to assess the general design objectives of each project and ensure that the objectives comply with both the Comprehensive Plan and the Development Objectives.[14]

The city's legislation does not specify prescribed guidelines for the urban designers to follow. The BRA has been given discretionary power to ensure that Boston's urban development objectives will be observed. The discretionary power has also been transferred to some degree to the BRA urban designers. This means that the urban designers' recommendations and views are highly respected and are taken quite seriously by the upper level BRA officials and the city's Zoning Board and Building Department.

No specific design review guidelines have been stipulated by the BRA or included in the City of Boston Zoning Ordinance. Instead, design review guidelines are established individually for each development and tailored to that project. The BRA urban design staff and a project's developer and architect establish criteria cooperatively in early design review sessions. Such guidelines are based upon urban development goals and policies of the city of Boston and the lessons learned from the previous development projects. I will demonstrate how well this procedure works in practice in Chapter 9.

The scope of issues covered in Boston's design reviews concentrates on detailed design of the individual buildings. Materials used, architectural design, aesthetics, and public amenities are among the items assessed by BRA urban designers. All issues of siting, massing, and compatibility are incorporated into the city's zoning regulations. There are two major issues of concern: preserving the distinctive characteristics of neighborhoods, as well as judging the compatibility of new development with the surrounding environment. Thus, when BRA urban designers evaluate proposed projects, they look at the project comprehensively and try to determine whether realistic urban design principles will be applied and whether the proposed building will meet the public's needs and desires.

The discretionary authority which the BRA has over all projects in Boston's urban redevelopment area enables the BRA to specify what each project should include. This specification takes place through numerous informal design review sessions between BRA urban designers and the developer and architect of the project. Furthermore, the BRA is involved with development projects which are built on private land. In these cases, both the BRA and the Zoning Board of Appeals are involved in the design review process. The following illustrates how the BRA, the Zoning Board of Appeals, and the design review sessions encourage development which will be based upon Boston's overall urban development policies.

The BRA owns all urban redevelopment land in Boston and consequently has the authority to review all proposed projects on urban renewal sites. However, if a developer has an uncomplicated project which he wants to build on privately owned land in downtown Boston, he may go directly to the Building Department and apply for a building permit instead of consulting with BRA. A building permit is issued so long as the developer's project is in complete compliance with city ordinances. However, the Building Department will reject the project if a variance is needed and will, instead, issue the developer a letter of refusal which lists the reasons for denying the building permit. Then the developer goes to the Secretary of the Board of Appeals with the letter, pays a fee, and makes an appointment for a public hearing. The size of the fee depends on the number of violations contained in the initial project plan.

The Building Commission sends the Board of Appeals, the BRA, and the Zoning Commission a copy of the developer's variance request.[15] The BRA receives a copy because it is required to submit a report with "recommendations, together with material, maps or plans to aid the Board of Appeal in judging the appeal."[16]

During the six to eight weeks it normally takes to schedule a public hearing, the developer and his architect will meet with BRA numerous times for informal design review sessions. The BRA recommends to the Board of Appeals whether the variance should be granted, so it is to the developer's advantage to seek BRA's advice. During the design review the developer can discuss his rationale for wanting a variance and perhaps persuade the BRA to recommend accepting the variance. The developer will often ask the BRA's opinion on his entire project during various design review meetings.

Prior to the BRA's submitting its recommendation to the Board of Appeals, a BRA planner will talk to some of the residents who live in the neighborhood where the project is planned to be built. Often the planner will try to arrange a community meeting to discuss neighborhood reaction to the project. Then the developer will go to see the BRA urban designer who is assigned to the neighborhood where the proposed project will be built. After the urban designer and developer go through several design reviews and negotiate problem areas in the project design, the BRA will send its recommendations to the Board of Appeals. After a variance has been granted, it must be used within two years, or it will become void.[17] If the variance is rejected, the developer cannot submit the same appeal to the "Board within one year after the adverse decision, except with the concurring vote of not less than four-fifths of the members."[18]

Often a developer may want to develop a private piece of land. As long as the land is not in an urban renewal zone, the developer is under no obligation to consult with BRA unless the project does not meet standards in the city's zoning ordinance. However, these standards are very restrictive and often prevent a developer from developing his land. In this situation, the developer usually appeals to the Zoning Board of Appeals for a variance; as discussed above, this will directly involve the BRA. Once again, the influence that BRA exerts on the final decision of the Board of Appeals will encourage the developer to go through numerous design reviews with BRA urban designers.

Boston's system of urban design is intended to encourage all developers and architects to go through design review sessions. The restrictive standards in the city's ordinance coupled with BRA's advisory role to the Board of Appeals practically ensures that all developers and architects will attend several design review sessions.

A special tax provision, Chapter 121A, has given the BRA the authority to negotiate real estate tax payments in Boston. Originally, Chapter 121A was established in order to stimulate new housing construction, but an amendment was passed which permitted commercial properties to qualify for the 121A tax agreement, as well.

The BRA Board, which has the power to approve 121A applications, has had no objections to granting 121A status for the construction of low and moderate income subsidized housing, since this use serves a clear public purpose.[19] Recently, however, the BRA has become more reluctant to approve 121A office projects. The tax agreement for office buildings limits the dividends of the corporation stock's par value, but "provides for fifteen years' exemption from taxation on real and personal property,"[20] an amount far below what would be paid if the property were subject to regular taxation. Several members of the Board, as well as organized interest groups, have argued that this in fact shifts an unfair burden of taxation to the homeowner in Boston. Consequently, Chapter 121A has been labeled a "tax dodge" which benefits only wealthy corporations. In defense of using Chapter 121A for commercial property, Robert Kenney, former BRA Director, stated in 1975:

> It is the present policy of the city, and one which I have strongly
> advocated, along with the mayor and assessors in order to
> encourage development. We would not consider it a tax dodge.[21]

All Chapter 121A developments are subject to BRA design review, a public hearing, and BRA Board approval before the application will be sent to the mayor for final approval. Thus, provision 121A serves to increase the clout the BRA has over development in the city of Boston.

Notes

1. Patricia Brady (n.d.). *The City of Boston: History, Planning, and Development* (Boston, Mass.: Boston Redevelopment Authority), pp. 2–3.

2. Robert J. Ryan (1979). "Boston Rediscovered," *Challenge Magazine*, 10:16.

3. John L. Kriken and Irene Perlis Torrey (1973). *Developing Urban Design Mechanisms* (Chicago: American Society of Planning Officials), p. 12.

4. Brady (n.d.), p. 4.

5. Kenneth Halpern (1978). *Downtown USA: Urban Design in Nine American Cities* (New York: Whitney Library of Design), p. 183.

6. Kriken and Torrey (1973), p. 12.

7. Boston Redevelopment Authority (1980). *BRA Fact Book.* (Boston), p. 3.

8. Boston Redevelopment Authority (1967). *The Design Review Process and Redeveloper's Architectural Submissions for Housing Parcels* (Boston: BRA Urban Design Department).

9. *Ibid.*

10. *Ibid.*

11. *Ibid.*

12. *Ibid.*

13. An example of a "restrictive" standard is the requirement that all downtown Boston projects have a FAR of 10. This prohibits the developer from making a profit and therefore dissuades him from building in the area—unless he works through BRA procedures.

14. Boston Redevelopment Authority (1980).

15. *City of Boston Zoning Ordinance* (1964). Section 5-4, p. 23.

16. *Ibid.*

17. *Ibid.*, Section 7-1, p. 30.

18. *Ibid.*, Section 5-3, p. 23.

19. Anthony J. Yudis (1975). "121A Looms Larger with Full Valuation," *Boston Sunday Globe*, March 16: Section A, p. 49.

20. Boston Redevelopment Authority (1980), p. 6.

21. Yudis (1975).

4
Concept Plan Review, Minneapolis

In 1976, Minnesota passed the Metropolitan Land Planning Act which required that the 189 communities in the Twin Cities Metropolitan Area adopt a comprehensive plan that was consistent with the area's regional plans. The following excerpt describes Minneapolis's objectives for initiating the development of a comprehensive plan:

> to prepare a plan which took neighborhood and community concerns into consideration . . . and [to provide a plan] which was useful for influencing day-to-day decisions about City development . . . The content . . . has been shaped and supplemented by local concerns about economic development, fiscal conditions, health, social services and other needs—the concerns of Minneapolis residents.[1]

The Concept Plan Review, incorporated into Minneapolis's Zoning Ordinance in 1976, echoes the same concerns as the Metropolitan Land Planning Act. The Concept Plan Review, which applies exclusively to townhouses and apartment developments of ten or more dwellings, is intended to ensure that proposed developments are compatible with the surrounding area by mandating that the City Planning Commission review and approve all proposed multi-dwelling residential units proposed for Minneapolis.[2]

Minneapolis's long-term plans for the 1980s are based on the goal of "keeping the people who live here [Minneapolis] now, and their offspring" in the city.[3] Thus, population stability is an immediate concern of Minneapolis public officials. In particular, Minneapolis wants to: 1) retain middle- and upper-income persons living in the city now, particularly young families, and 2) attract middle and upper income persons to the city.[4] The Concept Plan

Review is, therefore, a significant planning tool for the city and will likely become more important in the 1980s.

The Concept Plan Review procedures include a brief discussion of its intent followed by a list of guidelines for the developer to follow. Specific steps of the review process, such as meeting with the Planning and Development Department, submitting a concept plan, and attending a neighborhood meeting and a public hearing, are mentioned in the zoning booklet and in the city zoning ordinance in detail.[5] But even more detailed information will be given to the developer and his architect during the review sessions. The city zoning ordinance does state that the Concept Plan Review is mandatory for all residential developments that have ten or more dwelling units; and the developer and his architect must rely on information in existing zoning ordinances to prepare their project proposal.

The approach of the Concept Plan Review is best characterized as semidiscretionary because the developer relies on existing regulations contained in the city zoning ordinance to prepare his project proposal. The urban designers of the Planning and Development Department have only limited discretion to alter the ordinances; however, the ordinances have very flexible standards which are updated as the needs and the desires of the city change. This practice of updating the city zoning ordinance with the latest design techniques makes the zoning ordinance a practical and useful mechanism for effective urban design.

The review members of the Planning and Development Department are concerned primarily with three-dimensional design issues, the relationships of the buildings, and overall environmental quality. After a developer submits a plan to the Planning and Development Department, the urban designers review the plan to ensure that it meets all the qualifications specified in the city zoning ordinance. During this process, the urban designers have the authority to make specific decisions concerning standards which apply to the project under review. The review members' perception of the proposed project's compatibility with the environment greatly influences the members' recommendation concerning a proposed project. The Concept Plan Review is a formal design process because it is mandated in the city zoning ordinance.

The Concept Plan Review outlines the design review process in detail; however, the guidelines themselves are flexible in order to be applicable in all situations. The guidelines in the Concept Plan Review are not stated in prescriptive terms. Rather, they consist of lists of items that the developer must include in his initial concept plan. For instance, the concept plan must include the following items: height of building, number of units, lot size, land coverage, parking provisions, landscaping, changes in the area—such as road closing or tree removal, a three-dimensional sketch of the proposed project and its surroundings, access routes, expected rents or sales prices, a projected time schedule, information about the target population, demonstration of the need of the proposed service, and environmental impacts.[6] Urban designers of the Planning and Development Department provide the developer and his architect with prescriptive design criteria during the design review.

The guidelines explicitly state that the developer must meet first with the Zoning Administrator who "advises the applicant that he must go through a concept plan review process conducted by the Planning and Development Department."[7] The guidelines also instruct the developer to contact the Planning and Development Department.

Unlike many zoning codes, this document mentions the functions of various members of the review board. For example, before he even contacts the Zoning Administrator for an application review, a developer knows that the Planning and Development Department will receive his initial plan, set up and conduct a neighborhood meeting, and make recommendations about his proposed plan to the City Planning Commission. Thus, the guidelines enable the developer to know what is expected of him during all of the stages of the review process. The intent of the Concept Plan Review, therefore, is to inform the developer of the essence of the Concept Plan Review procedures and to provide him with more substantive information during the review sessions with the Planning and Development Department.

The guidelines in the Minneapolis Concept Plan Review procedure focus on the review process itself, rather than on architectural details, massing, and frontage issues. The primary issues of concern are "to ensure a satisfactory relationship of the proposed development compatible with the character of the surrounding neighborhood."[8] The scope of the manual includes the full spectrum of issues related to urban development, but the guidelines do not specify any specific criteria which the developer and his architect must meet. The guidelines only list the issues which must be included in the initial concept plan and indicate that the developer must participate in a concept plan review,[9] attend a neighborhood meeting,[10] and hold a public hearing.[11]

Since the guidelines provide the developer with information on the process of the review sessions, they can be characterized as procedural rather than substantive guidelines. The city's zoning ordinances contain all of the prescriptive standards which the developer and his architect will need to prepare their project plan; these regulations are interpreted for the developer and his architect by the urban designers during the design review sessions. The first session is scheduled prior even to submission of the initial preliminary plans to the Planning and Development Department.

Within two weeks after the initial concept plan has been submitted to the Planning and Development staff, a neighborhood meeting with the property owners who live within 200 feet of the proposed site is conducted. Both the developer and the Planning Department must provide information for this meeting, and it is the responsibility of the Planning and Development Department staff to keep records of the meeting.[12] Again, the developer and his architect may have several informal design review sessions with urban designers and planners from the Planning and Development Department before the meeting. Within one month after the neighborhood meeting, the City Planning Commission holds a public hearing. People who went to the neighborhood meeting as well as any other interested party may attend the public hearing. If by chance the time between the neighborhood meeting and the public hearing is more than one month, a second neighborhood meeting must be held.[13]

The developer presents his concept plan at the public hearing, and the Planning and Development Department presents an evaluation of that plan. If the Planning and Development Department staff suggest that a technical advisory committee composed of urban designers and planners examine the concept plan prior to the hearing, the committee's recommendations must also be presented at the hearing.[14] The Planning and Development

Department will then send a report to the City Planning Commission.

The City Planning Commission then makes recommendations about the project to the City Council, and the City Council has 30 days from the time of the public hearing to vote favorably or unfavorably on the concept plan. If the City Council approves the plan, the developer may then prepare final plans and submit them to "the department of inspections within one year of the date of the concept plan approval."[15] The Zoning Administrator reviews the final plans to ensure that they are consistent with the initial concept plan. As long as the two plans are consistent, the Zoning Administrator approves the plan. If the Zoning Administrator finds inconsistencies between the two plans, he must reject the plan; however, the developer has the option to appeal the Zoning Administrator's decision to the City Council within 15 days after notification of the refusal. The City Council may reverse the prior decision with a majority vote.[16]

5

Fifth Avenue Special District Design Review, New York City

New York City first attempted to improve urban design in 1961 by revising its zoning ordinance. The establishment of incentive zoning as part of a major reworking of the ordinance enabled developers to increase the floor area of a building up to 20% in certain downtown areas if a public amenity such as a plaza or arcade met the qualifications of the ordinance. While this was a step in the right direction, the incentive zoning ordinance of 1961 did not encourage cohesive planning and urban design; instead, buildings were examined individually rather than in the context of their immediate surroundings and with regard to their interrelationships with existing buildings. The passage of time demonstrated that the 1961 incentive zoning would be more effective in less-developed areas than in dense inner city of New York.

In an attempt to gain additional control over then-current trends of development in New York City, Mayor John Lindsay created a Committee on Urban Design in 1966 which was headed by William S. Paley. This committee conducted numerous studies and recommended that an urban design group be included within the City Planning Department staff. Shortly after the release of this recommendation, an urban design function (The Urban Design Group) was incorporated into the City Planning Department.[1]

An outgrowth of the 1961 zoning incentive idea was the establishment of "Special Zoning Districts." These special districts consist of specific areas with zoning regulations that are tailored to their particular characteristics and uses in New York City. Developers are required to include certain public amenities the city wants in their building plans rather than simply being told what they cannot do. Additionally, there are other features which the developer has the option to include in his plan and, if they are included, he is awarded extra floor space in return.

The special zoning district approach to controlling urban development was applied to Fifth Avenue in 1971, the sixth such special district since their initial establishment in 1967. Prior to creating the Fifth Avenue Special District (hereafter referred to as FASD), both the public and private sectors of New York City were concerned over the changing character of Fifth Avenue. Luxury retail shops located on the ground floors of the buildings were being replaced by domestic and foreign banks, airline ticket offices, and other nonretail uses. The sheer prestige of Fifth Avenue attracted these institutions: the numerous and affluent shoppers on the Avenue were incentives for domestic banks to locate there; foreign banks sought this location as a means of identifying themselves; and airlines and corporations were after the prestige and advertising potential offered by a Fifth Avenue location.[2] This influx of institutional uses on Fifth Avenue occured at such a rapid rate that by 1971 retailers occupied only 55% of Fifth Avenue frontage.[3] Then-current zoning regulations perpetuated the situation and encouraged the construction of buildings that were not integrated with existing structures on the Avenue.

At this point in time it became increasingly clear to the citizenry of New York City that unless something was done, Fifth Avenue could end up like Sixth Avenue—lined with "plazas, fountains, banks, showrooms and glass lobbies . . . different in shape and size from each other"[4]. The City Planning Commission then decided to devise a special district for Fifth Avenue which would "make sure that the new Fifth Avenue would continue to be a great shopping center . . . and that enough people would be brought in to live so that the street would stay alive 24 hours a day."[5]

Former Mayor Lindsay, one of the key supporters of such a zoning ordinance, encouraged Jaquelin Robertson, Director of the city's Office of Midtown Planning and Development, to devise an urban plan to control the undesirable side effects of current regulations.[6] Much time and effort went into the preparation of the FASD. For instance, the Office of Midtown Planning and Development ran a study entitled "The Impact of the Fifth Avenue Special District Legislation of Retail Floor Space on Fifth Avenue" to identify possible effects of the proposed zoning ordinance.[7]

Public and private organizations such as the Real Estate Board of New York, the Fifth Avenue Association, the Citizens Housing and Planning Council, the Municipal Arts Society, and the editorial staff of *The New York Times* also took an active role in supporting the FASD zoning proposal.[8] It should also be noted that political undercurrents, in addition to the obvious physical considerations, led to the creation of the FASD. Political factors, in fact, provided the initial impetus for the Office of Midtown Planning and Development's interest in Fifth Avenue. The Department of City Planning acknowledged two of the major political issues:

1. To satisfy the Fifth Avenue Association that the City is concerned about the future of retailing on the Avenue and is taking positive action to restore its vitality; and

2. To counteract the public's impression that the City is "falling apart." The flight of major corporate headquarters to the suburbs together with the closing of several major Fifth Avenue stores produced the impression that the City was in a state of accelerated deterioration. Such an impression impaired the Mayor's image and reputation as an effective urban official.[9]

Given the rapidly changing nature of Fifth Avenue and the concern it drew from the public and private sectors, it is not surprising that the FASD was voted into law by the Board of Estimate with relatively little opposition. On March 26, 1971, the FASD was included in the City of New York Zoning Ordinance.

The FASD is intended to inform developers of the type of development the city is interested in promoting on Fifth Avenue. It encourages developers to plan new developments which comply with the distinct needs of the district—increasing retail and residential facilities and public amenities—by providing information on the required uses and basic design of a building.

The document containing the ordinance begins with a discussion of the general purpose and provisions of this special district, followed by a description of the regulations. The sections of this chapter are organized by using major and minor category headings. Categories are broken down into mutually exclusive issues, such as Mandatory Use Regulations and Prohibitions, Special Regulations for Residential of Hotel Floor Area Bonus, Mandatory Lot Improvement Regulations and Prohibitions, Elective Lot Improvements, and Special Regulations for Lot Coverage. Most of the categories list several standards and often contain two or more subcategories.[10]

The FASD can be classified as a more decentralized approach to

urban design and planning because its regulations apply exclusively to this section of the city.[11] The regulations contained in this
document are comprehensive and laid out in great detail. As stated
earlier, the FASD is a unique approach to urban design because
incentives in the form of floor area bonuses are included. Thus, if a
developer incorporates a through-block connection, subway connection, a plaza, landscaped terrace, or a covered pedestrian space
in the development, a bonus in floor area of between two and
fourteen square feet for each square foot of public amenity is
awarded to the developer, equivalent to a 20% FAR increase.[12] In
addition, the developer may add another 20% of FAR and increase
his lot coverage by 10% by including more residential, hotel, and
retail uses in his building, as specified in the regulations.[13]

The primary intention of the FASD is that it be self-administering, but this intent is rarely realized because developers have the
prerogative to include one or more options in their development
plans. This option consequently requires them to go through a
planning review procedure. The length of the design review
depends on the scale of the development and the cooperation of
the developer. The following discussion will clarify why the FASD
is a semi-self-administering approach to design review which may
require a planning review as well.

The regulations outlined in the FASD are very descriptive and
self-explanatory. Note, however, that the legislation does not
mandate that developers and their architects attend design review
sessions; in fact, the regulations do not even mention that the
Office of Midtown Planning and Development has a highly
qualified technical staff capable of advising the developers of
efficient ways to incorporate the regulations and bonus system in
their plans. Clearly, it is left to the discretion of the developer to
decide whether to use the FASD incentive regulations or to build
"as of right" within the FASD guidelines.

Three requirements in the FASD legislation must be followed by
all developers who plan to build in this special district. First, "the
front wall of all developments within the special district shall
extend along the entire length of the street line for a minimum
height of three stories."[14] This regulation applies to all zoning lots
greater than 100 feet in depth from the streetline.[15] Second, "uses
on the ground floor, or within 5 feet of curb level, shall be limited
to retail uses."[16] Even if the developer prefers to build "as of right,"
he must build on the property line of Fifth Avenue and provide

retail use at the ground level of the building which faces Fifth Avenue. Third, "any development located within the Special District shall contain not less than a floor area ratio equivalent to 1.00."[17] As long as the developers comply with these three requirements, they can bypass the Office of Midtown Planning and Development (OMPD, the urban design body for Midtown), use the guidelines outlined in the FASD and the City Ordinance to prepare a plan, and submit an application to the Building Department for a building permit. Thus in this case, the approach is self-administering.

Often, however, developers may want to apply for a special permit which will allow them to modify specific zoning regulations. In order to apply for such a special permit, developers must go through a formal planning review session called the "Uniform Land Use Review Procedure."[18] The City Planning Commission, which is advisory to the Board of Estimate, and the Board of Estimate itself have the power to reject the special permit if the variance does not "enhance the relationship of the building to nearby buildings."[19] To this end, the FASD is a self-administering approach to design review but requires planning review as well. Therefore, the FASD is more appropriately described as a semi-self-administering approach, depending whether the developer exercises his right to request a special permit.

The guidelines presented in this document are stated in prescriptive terms, with the majority of the standards stated concisely and containing ample specifications. For instance, one guideline states that developers are eligible for a floor area bonus if "a terrace is located at the roof of the sixth story or at the 85 foot level, or below and above a height of three stories."[21] However, some additional conditions which must be met to qualify for the bonus are less exact and more performance-oriented so as to give the architects greater design freedom: landscape at least 25% of the terrace area and provide benches and walking space.[22] It is up to the developers to choose, at their own discretion, the type of landscaping and the number of benches to include for the terrace in this case. Other standards are stated ambiguously, and so interpretation may vary substantially for each developer. For example, "the terrace area is readily accessible to the public at least during normal business hours" may have different meanings for different developers.[23]

Overall, the guidelines give sufficient direction on how to

develop an acceptable plan. Issues such as minimum retail space requirements, restrictions on ground floor uses, and covered pedestrian space requirements are explicitly outlined in prescriptive guidelines. The requirements to qualify for bonus FAR are also clearly stated—specific numbers are given for the exact amount of residential and retail use a developer must include in his building to qualify for a specified amount of bonus floor space.

The issues of concern in the FASD deal with preserving the distinct character of the Avenue by increasing retail and residential facilities and public amenities on Fifth Avenue; hence, the scope of legislation covers elements relative to the placement and structure of a building and the type of activity the building may be used for. With respect to physical design, the content of the regulations is focused on the heights of buildings, their distance from one another, their frontages, and their location on Fifth Avenue. A number of the standards are mandatory—specific setbacks for developments on Fifth Avenue, minimum retail space required in each building, no mass placed within 50 feet of the street line, and no off-street parking facilities.[24] Amenities considered less essential, such as through-block connections, covered pedestrian spaces, plazas, landscaped terraces,[25] additional residential and hotel use in buildings,[26] are optional, though encouraged by the incentive bonuses available to developers who include these amenities in their plans. The bonuses allow a developer to add additional floor space to his building by following the provisions of the District, but the extra floor area over 18.0 FAR must be used for residential space and not for offices.

Let us now examine how the FASD works. All buildings in the District must satisfy the mandatory requirements of the legislation, including the provision of 1 FAR in retail (see Fig. 5-1, A). The developer may build up to 15 FAR, and 14 FAR of the total may be used for office, residential, or hotel space. If the developer includes Elective Lot Improvements in the building, he will be given a 20% bonus; thus the FAR increases to 18. Again, the developer has the option of choosing the use for all of the floor area except for 1.0 FAR in retail (see Fig. 5-1, B). In order for the developer to take advantage of the bonus incentives provided in the FASD legislation, he must first meet all the requirements indicated in Figure 5-1, A and B. That is, up to 18 FAR of the floor area can be used for office, residential, retailing, or hotel use. By providing additional retail and residential space in the building, the developer is awarded a 20% bonus, thus increasing the building total FAR to 21.6. The legislation requires that only the last 20% increment (18 FAR to 21.6 FAR) be in residential or hotel uses (see Fig. 5-1, C).

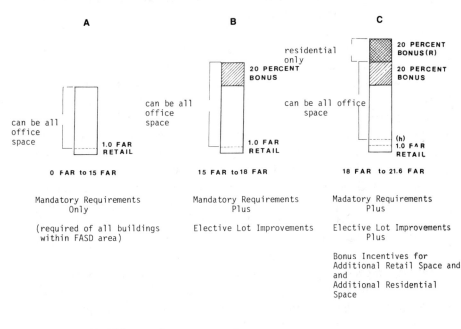

Figure 5–1: Application of FASD Guidelines

OMPD's Lauren Otis has stated that contrary to ordinary zoning, the FASD is only involved with zoning as a process.[27] The regulations apply solely to privately owned land, and a developer is not mandated to go through a design review process before he receives a building permit. For example, if a developer decides to develop a site of land on Fifth Avenue, he can use the guidelines contained in the FASD to prepare a plan which is in compliance with the district regulations. The regulations in the document also include specific modifications such as increases in coverage or inclusion of a public amenity in exchange for additional FAR which the developer may include in his plan. These options are explained in detail in the regulations, and so long as the developer remains in compliance with FASD guidelines, he need not receive authority from the City Planning Commission to adopt these modifications. This is a circumstance already noted under which the developer submits his plans to the Building Department, during which time staff members of the Building Department examine the plan to determine if it is in compliance with the FASD guidelines. The developer is required to attend reviews conducted by the Building Department; he subsequently receives a building permit so long as his plan complies with the regulations in the FASD.

However, if the developer wishes to include modifications in his building plans which vary from the legislation, he must submit an application requesting approval of the changes to the City Planning Commission (hereafter referred to as CPC). Any changes which are granted to the developer in lieu of the regulations in the text must be incorporated as additional standards in the FASD. That is, the legislation must be revised to include any modifications that the CPC approves so that future developers will employ these newly approved standards in their plans. Including these modifications in the legislation benefits all parties involved: the legislation becomes a better zoning document because it incorporates (as Otis stated) "more design elements into it;"[28] the buildings are better designed and therefore may increase public enjoyment; and future developers will undoubtedly save time by not having to apply for a similar modification in the future.

When a developer is interested in this modification in standards so as to exceed limits as defined in the FASD, he must go through a discretionary zoning process called "Uniform Land Use Review Procedure," which is the same process required for all zoning ordinance changes. This process involves numerous steps. First, the developer draws up a preliminary set of plans and submits them, along with an application, to the CPC. The CPC staff reviews the plans to ensure that all aspects of the FASD have been met and then makes comments about the requested modifications. Often the CPC consults with the Office of Midtown Planning and Development. It is, therefore, to the developer's advantage to have many design review sessions with OMPD even though OMPD is only advisory to the CPC. The developer has the opportunity to point out to OMPD that his requests are an improvement over current regulations and will ultimately benefit future Fifth Avenue development; perhaps then, the OMPD, after an independent analysis, may voice a positive opinion of the modifications to the CPC. Even if this is not the case, it benefits the developer to consult with the OMPD because this organization can help the developer design the modifications in such a way to increase the probability of their being accepted by the CPC. Furthermore, the OMPD can also offer advice on how to comply with all the technical regulations in FASD and to take advantage of the bonus system efficiently.

After the CPC reviews and comments on the requested modifications, the Community Board reviews the changes, publicly announces the project, holds a public hearing, and finally votes favorably or unfavorably on the changes. An in-house committee often reviews the developer's proposal with the developer and provides recommendations to the Community Board. This whole segment of the discretionary zoning process takes place within 60 days. The Community Board then returns the plans, its comments, and its vote to the CPC. After another public hearing is held, the CPC examines the project in detail and looks at the whole building again. The commission also reviews the comments and vote of the Community Board before making a final vote on the project. The CPC must vote within 60 days after receiving the Community Board's comments.

The Board of Estimate then receives a detailed report from the CPC which outlines the CPC's viewpoint on the project. The way the CPC voted and justifications for the action are included in this report. For example, if the vote is positive, the CPC discusses why it feels the change would be an improvement over the current standards in the FASD. Regardless of the CPC's vote, the report always includes comments and positions viewed in the public hearing.

The Board of Estimate has 60 days to hold another public hearing, review the report from the CPC, and make a final vote on the project. If the Board of Estimate fails to approve the plan, the developer receives his plan back along with explanations for the rejection. If the plan receives a favorable vote, the set of plans that are filed for this change are sent to the Building Department. When the developer's architect applies for a building permit from the Building Department, the Building Department officials, instead of going through normal zoning review processes, simply pick up the plans sent by the Board of Estimate and see whether the two sets of plans match. As long as the two sets of plans are identical, the Building Department issues a building permit. If the developer wishes to make a change in his plan at a later date, he must go through the whole process again if it is a major change, such as adding another floor. If it is a minor change, he is allowed to file the change directly with the Building Department.

As alluded to throughout this section, there is no formal design review process as a part of the FASD. The developer and his architect have the option to consult with the OMPD if they wish and may schedule as many informal design review sessions as they feel necessary. The discussion above illustrates that it is to the advantage of the developer and his architect to meet with the OMPD. Even if they choose to comply totally with the regulations in the FASD, the OMPD can interpret any ambiguous regulations and explain how the developer and his architect can best take advantage of the regulations and bonuses. If the developer and his architect wish to apply for a special permit, the design review becomes even more valuable because the staff of OMPD can again explain various regulations and also offer suggestions on what type of variance is most likely to be approved. Furthermore, during the planning review sessions when the requested variances are examined, the CPC often seeks the advice of the design review staff. If the OMPD has prior knowledge of the special permit request, that urban design body is in better position to support the request and offer insight as to why this variance is indeed an improvement over the present regulations.

Although the design review is not formal, it may be considered necessary in all situations except those when the developer does not wish to incorporate bonuses in his plan, but this situation seldom occurs. When the design review is fully utilized, it is beneficial to both the developer and his architect and simultaneously provides benefits to the public, since the OMPD concentrates primarily on issues relative to public concerns.

Notes

1. Peter Blake (1971). "The New Fifth Avenue," *New York Magazine*, January.

2. Robert E. Davis and Jon Weston, eds. (1975). *The Special Zoning Concept in New York City* (New York: New School for Social Research, Center for New York City Affairs).

3. Robert Ponte (1971). "The Changing Locational Pattern of Community Activity in Midtown Manhattan." Ph.D. dissertation, Columbia University.

4. Blake (1971).

5. *Ibid.*

6. *Ibid.*

7. Ponte (1971).

8. *Ibid.*

9. New York City Department of City Planning (1971). *Memorandum,* "Fifth Avenue Critical Issues," January 19, pp. 5–6.

10. *City of New York Zoning Ordinance* (1975). Special Fifth Avenue District, Chapter 7, Sections 87–03 through 87–08, pp. 415–418.

11. John L. Kriken and Irene Perlis Torrey (1973). *Developing Urban Design Mechanisms* (Chicago: American Society of Planning Officials), p. 9.

12. *City of New York Zoning Ordinance* (1975). Special Fifth Avenue District, Chapter 7, Section 87–065, p. 417.

13. *Ibid.,* Sections 87–08 and 87–09, p. 418.

14. *Ibid.,* Section 87–05, p. 415.

15. *Ibid.*

16. *Ibid.,* Section 87–032, p. 413.

17. *Ibid.*

18. A complete description of this process is included in Chapter 10 of this book.

19. *City of New York Zoning Ordinance* (1975). Special Fifth Avenue District, Chapter 7, Section 87–102, (ii), p. 419.

20. *Ibid.,* (iii), p. 419.

21. *Ibid.,* Section 87–064, p. 418.

22. *Ibid.,* (a + b), p. 418.

23. *Ibid.,* (c), p. 418.

24. *Ibid.,* Sections 87–05, 87–031, 87–032, 87–041, and 87–043, pp. 415, 413, 413, 414, 414 respectively.

25. *Ibid.,* Section 87–06, p. 415.

26. *Ibid.,* Section 87–08, p. 418.

27. Lauren Otis (1979). Personal conversation, December 19.

28. *Ibid.*

6

Urban Design Review, San Francisco

Before 1972, San Francisco did not have a comprehensive city-wide master plan to address urban design issues; but this was not unusual—it was virtually impossible to find any major city with a city-wide urban design plan in 1970.[1] The need for a comprehensive urban design plan to deal with "the sensuous, aesthetic, and visual qualities of the urban environment"[2] in San Francisco was growing among government officials and citizen groups alike. People were becoming increasingly concerned over monotonous street facades, new buildings out of scale with existing buildings, and the proliferation of parking lots. By the late 1960s, conflicts over building projects interfering with the unique natural and man-made qualities of San Francisco—the hills, the water, the open space, special architectural features, and environmental areas—prompted the staff of the Planning Department to begin working on a city-wide urban design study and plan.[3]

Allan Jacobs, Director of the City Planning Department from 1967 through 1974, set up an urban design and planning staff in the latter part of 1968 to conduct the study. The Citizens Advisory Committee, composed of architects, economists, businessmen, government officials, planning commissioners, interest groups, and others with knowledge of San Francisco, offered the city planners advice and criticism throughout the study. Eight preliminary reports were published by the planning staff during the three-year study period. Each report represented different stages in the formulation of San Francisco's urban design plans and policies. The purpose of these preliminary reports was to inform the public and civic leaders of what the planners were doing, solicit comments and opinions on the content of the study, and generally involve the public in urban design matters.[4] Feedback generated by the public enabled the city planners to formulate urban design policies which were more responsive to citizen concerns. In 1971, the Urban Design Plan was adopted as part of the city's Master Plan.[5]

The urban designers of the City Planning Department organize and conduct the urban design review process, thus centralizing the City Planning Department's review of the most important development projects. The designers use the technical advice of other staff members in addition to their own design expertise. The central concern of the review is "urban design," and the aspects covered are Landscape and Environment, Relationships to Structures and Open Spaces, Circulation, Protection of Neighborhoods, and Compliance with Other Regulations. These criteria are fully discussed in Preliminary Report Number 7, *Implementation Approaches*.[6] To a great extent the Urban Design Plan serves as a design manual for this process, and in some cases more specific guidelines serve to supplement the plan; examples of the latter are the written specifications for parking lots and fast-food outlets.[7] An average of 100 projects go through review each year, but only 40 projects are carried as far as the building permit application stage.[8] Although the Urban Design Review has a city-wide application, it is primarily directed towards the downtown development projects, major housing projects, and areas designated by the Urban Design Plan as "special" or "sensitive" areas.

Design review in San Francisco is semidiscretionary in nature. The recommendations of the urban designers and planners of the Department of City Planning exert influence on the City Planning Commission's (CPC) decision in many cases. The CPC has the legal authority to reject or accept a proposed project:

> Under the Charter and Municipal Code, the City Planning
> Commission is empowered to exercise a broad power of
> discretionary review where the public interest would be seriously
> endangered by a contemplated building project.[9]

Urban design review is an informal process in San Francisco in which the Urban Design Plan serves as a framework, but in a few cases the design review process is considered formal. For instance, Resolution No. 6111, adopted by the CPC in June 1967, requires the Commission to review all new and enlarged buildings along

Market Street.[10] Normally, however, urban design reviews in San Francisco are informal. Whether the design review is formal or informal, San Francisco's urban designers and planners of the Department of City Planning serve in an advisory capacity during the numerous informal design review sessions. In addition, the technical advice that the Department of City Planning's urban designers provide to the CPC, along with the discretionary authority which has been given to the CPC, ensures that San Francisco's urban development objectives will be achieved.

The Urban Design Plan included in the City Planning Code is stated "as city-wide guidelines in order to accommodate the present period of construction" taking place throughout San Francisco.[11] Thus, the plan is flexible so as to provide a design approach to the physical problems which often result when city development occurs.

The city-wide guidelines are intended to "provide a framework for more detailed urban design plans at the district and neighborhood levels;"[12] hence, the urban design guidelines are "specific where appropriate, but sufficiently general to be applied at the city-wide level."[13] Thus in this respect, the guidelines can be viewed as both city-wide and special district oriented. The guidelines are prescriptive in nature, but the generality of the standards necessitates that urban designers and planners of the Department of City Planning provide supplemental information to the developers and their architects during the design review. For instance, urban design guidelines for the height of buildings in the downtown designate ranges rather than specific heights. The guidelines are not height restrictions, but rather they "reflect the combined use of urban design principles, specific sets of design criteria, and the height of existing development."[14] Thus, during design reviews, discussion will focus first on the intent of the proposal before discussing specific design elements of the proposal. There are strict height limitations in neighborhood areas in San Francisco, and the city is currently developing performance guidelines and incentives to include in the Urban Design Plan.

Urban design guidelines for bulk of buildings is another example of San Francisco's attempt to design flexible urban development standards. For instance, building bulk guidelines for the downtown area recommend that the maximum length of a building wall not exceed 170 feet and the maximum horizontal dimension of a building on a diagonal not exceed 200 feet.[15] The authors of these guidelines feel that

> these dimensions . . . can apply to many different forms and shapes of buildings. As a result they are flexible and can apply to both present and future designs of buildings.[16]

Thus, San Francisco has adopted an overall Urban Design Plan which is used as a framework for the design review. Within this system urban designers have some discretion which is based on the flexibility of the plan. However, while the guidelines assist the developer and his architect in developing a project design, they must work with urban designers and planners of the Department of City Planning in order to obtain the substantive information they need to prepare an acceptable design.

In 1978, the Department of City Planning began drafting a booklet titled *Design Guidelines for Major New Developments: An Interpretation of the Goals and Policies of the San Francisco Urban Design Plan* which "will serve as a useful checklist of the most common design concerns."[17] This booklet is intended to supplement the Urban Design Plan by providing specific illustrations of ways selected design objectives may be achieved.

San Francisco's Urban Design Plan is intended "to preserve and protect portions of the city that are distinctive, fragile, and exceptional; and to recommend methods for enhancing sections of the city that do not share in these amenities."[18] The urban design review process *per se* is not mentioned in the City Planning Code, although a one-year interim control requires that proposed buildings in downtown San Francisco go through discretionary zoning procedures. The purpose of these controls is to facilitate

> careful review of any development proposal which would increase the total amount of space and activities in this area [the downtown area], and through such review to prevent the construction of any development which is inappropriate for the City. . . . The City Planning Commission has the authority to conduct discretionary reviews of building permit applications under a power vested in the Commission . . . and that power is exercised in cases in which the proposed development meets the literal requirements of the City Planning Code but may nevertheless have serious detrimental effects. . . .[19]

The Urban Design Plan's issues of concern concentrate on two major aspects of urban design: "the underlying nature base" of the city and the way the city "has been developed upon its natural base."[20] Contrary to typical city planning which is concerned primarily with meeting the social, political, and economic needs of urban residents, urban design in San Francisco deals with "visual qualities of the environment."[21]

The scope of issues covered in the urban Design Plan centers on 10 urban design aspects which are basic to all urban design goals in San Francisco. The "rules" or "principles" range from functional to aesthetic concerns and are found in varying degrees in all proposed projects. They are amenity/comfort, visual interests, activity, clarity and convenience, character/distinctiveness, definition of space, views, variety/contrast, harmony/compatibility, and scale and pattern—the fundamental concerns of urban design in San Francisco. These provide the basic measurements by which proposed projects are evaluated.[22] The intent of these principles is to modify each other: "the objective to achieve variety and contrast, for example, is modified in degree by the concern to harmonize with existing scale or other quality of an area."[23] These 10 principles look at functional and aesthetic components of urban design and the effect they may have on the public's perception of the city and consequently on the public's actions within the city. That is, the public will not use city facilities unless they are physically appealing and convenient to get to.

San Francisco is interested in creating "rich street life" so as to enhance the pedestrian experience.[24] Thus, the guidelines look at both large and small elements of proposed developments in San Francisco in order to identify elements which will enhance both physical development and facility utilization in San Francisco. For example, from a functional standpoint, the guidelines encourage retail use at the ground level of buildings since stores are principal generators of street activities and at the same time discourage extensive use of office lobbies in shopping areas because they detract from visual interest[25] and thereby may discourage people from using the facilities. The guidelines are also highly concerned with aesthetic concerns such as increasing the visual quality of pedestrian amenities, making the urban environment visually pleasing by including detailed facades and intricate entries in buildings.[26] The type of materials, colors, and textures of buildings are also included in the guidelines. These kinds of external details are consistent and compatible with the traditional type of buildings in many sections of San Francisco and therefore enhance the visual quality of San Francisco's urban design.

The Urban Design Plan includes issues relating to height, bulk, use, and size of the buildings, treatment of frontage, access to public spaces, protecting street views and space, preserving natural land features, architectural design, and open space and landscaping. The Plan "looks at the city strictly from an urban design point of view [and] deals with the need and potential for improving the city's physical form and environment."[27] Approaching urban design review in this manner enables the city to provide the public with the amenities they most desire.

Prior to February 1980, developers who planned on building in downtown areas of San Francisco could obtain a building permit by building completely in accordance with the City Zoning Ordinance, by applying for Discretionary Zoning, or by going through Conditional Use Review. The recent interim control process mandating that all new developments in downtown San Francisco go through discretionary zoning consists of three separate reviews: the planning review, the environmental review, and the urban design review. It currently takes a minimum of 24 weeks to go through these three review processes.[28]

The developer first files an application with the Building Department; a copy of the designer's proposed project design must be included with this application. The Building Department then refers the proposed project to the urban designers and planners of the Department of City Planning who conduct many informal design review sessions with the developer and his architect. The planning review, environmental review, and urban design review all must take place before the Department of City Planning submits a recommendation to the City Planning Commission and states whether or not it feels a building permit should be issued.

Within the planning review, the urban designers and planners review the proposed project to ensure that the project complies with the written standards of the City Planning Code. The environmental review is mandated by the California Environmental Quality Act of 1970 for all projects.[29] The Department of City Planning has published a booklet which explains the format and content of a Draft Environmental Impact Report (DEIR) for projects that may have a significant effect on the environment.[30] The booklet indicates that:

the private applicant of the board, commission or department which is to carry out or approve the project must submit the data necessary for the DEIR to the Department of City Planning. Environmental Reviews are carried out by the Office of Environmental Review (OER) within the Department. The City and County of San Francisco is the legal author of the published document and assumes all responsibility for its content.[31]

Finally, urban designers and planners of the Department of City Planning conduct the urban design review with the developer and his architect.

The Department of City Planning submits its recommendations on the project to the City Planning Commission. The CPC places high regard on the Department of City Planning's recommendations of proposed projects. If the proposed project is accepted by the CPC, the proposal is then sent to the Building Department, and a building permit is issued. If the CPC rejects the project, the developer has the option of submitting the proposal to the Board of Permit Appeals. The Building Department issues a building permit if the Board accepts the proposal; however, if the Board rejects the plan, the developer has no recourse.

The urban designers and planners like to meet with developers and their architects "at an early stage" so that the "advice and persuasion" of the urban designers and planners can guide the developer and his architect in designing their project "rather than resorting to mandatory review powers."[32] Thus, numerous informal urban design review sessions with the urban designers and planners of the Department of City Planning prior to submitting an application to the Building Department are encouraged.

Notes

1. San Francisco Department of City Planning (1975). *Memorandum* to the City Planning Commission from Dean L. Macris, Director of Planning, March 13, p. 1.

2. Allan B. Jacobs (1978). *Making City Planning Work* (Chicago: American Society of Planning Officials), p. 216.

3. John L. Kriken and Irene Pearlis Torrey (1973). *Developing Urban Design Mechanisms* (Chicago: American Society of Planning Officials), p. 4.

4. Jacobs (1978), pp. 196–199.

5. *Ibid.*, p. 216.

6. San Francisco Department of City Planning (1970*a*). *Preliminary Report No. 7: Implementation Approaches* (Springfield, Va.: National Technical Information Service).

7. San Francisco Department of City Planning (1975), p. 9.

8. *Ibid.*

9. San Francisco Department of City Planning (1970*a*).

10. San Francisco Department of City Planning (1979*a*). *One Year Interim Control.*

11. San Francisco Department of City Planning (1970*b*). *Preliminary Report No. 8: Urban Design Plan* (Springfield, Va.: National Technical Information Service), p. 2.

12. *Ibid.*, p. 3.

13. *Ibid.*

14. *Ibid.*, p. 130.

15. *Ibid.*

16. San Francisco Department of City Planning (1971). *Urban Design Plan for the Comprehensive Plan of San Francisco*, p. V-9.

17. San Francisco Department of City Planning (1978). *Design Guidelines for Major New Developments: An Interpretation of the Goals and Policies of the San Francisco Urban Design Plan*, p. 1.

18. San Francisco Department of City Planning (1970*b*), p. 5.

19. San Francisco City Planning Commission (1980). Resolution No. 8474, p. 1.

20. San Francisco Department of City Planning (1970*b*), p. 5.

21. Jacobs (1978), p. 192.

22. San Francisco Department of City Planning (1970*c*). *Preliminary Report No. 5: Urban Design Principles for San Francisco* (Springfield, Va., Technical Information Service), pp. 3–4.

23. *Ibid.*, p. 4.

24. *Ibid.*, p. 13.

25. *Ibid.*

26. *Ibid.*, p. 16.

27. San Francisco Department of City Planning (1970*b*), p. 3.

28. San Francisco Department of City Planning, (1979*a*).

29. *California Environmental Quality Act* (1970). Chapter 5, Section 21160.

30. San Francisco Department of City Planning (1979*b*). *Format and Guidelines for Preparing an Environmental Impact Report*, p. 1.

31. *Ibid.*

32. San Francisco Department of City Planning (1975), p. 9.

7

Comparative Study and Classification of the Models

The models in Boston, Minneapolis, New York City, and San Francisco have been examined individually. The similarities and differences among these four models are illustrated in Figures 7-1 through 7-4. We now shall reexamine the approach, nature, elements, and management of each model respectively and contrast issues of major concern.

Approach

Many factors influence the approach a city selects to control design reviews. The attitude of the city officials and the general public, the economic climate of the city, the size and professional expertise of the design review staff, and the type of elements selected to be controlled are a few of the factors which are determinants of the design review approach adopted by a city. Figure 7-1 displays the various approaches used by the four models examined in this study.

The discretionary approach may be most appropriate or attractive when architectural details, which are not easily specified prior to preparing the design proposal, are the major issues of concern. In other instances, the discretionary approach may be

CITY	APPROACH							
	SELF - ADMINISTERING	SEMI SELF - ADMINISTERING	SEMI DISCRETIONARY	DISCRETIONARY	FORMAL	INFORMAL	PROJECT ORIENTED	PROCESS ORIENTED
BOSTON				●		●	●	
MINNEAPOLIS			●		●		●	
NEW YORK		●				●		●
SAN FRANCISCO			●		●	●	●	●

Figure 7-1: Design Review Approaches

most appropriate when the city is interested in preserving elements which are difficult to incorporate into standards. The broad guidelines used in BRA's design review describe some general directions of the guidelines but leave the measurement of acceptability to the discretion of the reviewer. Boston's decision to use the discretionary approach may be based upon the difficulty involved in writing guidelines that are effective in preserving the distinct character of each neighborhood in Boston, as well as ensuring that new developments are compatible with their surrounding environments. Furthermore, the BRA design review process is based on the understanding that each project is unique and should have a set of guidelines designed specifically to enhance the project's desirable effects on the city.

Boston's approach does exercise a highly centralized form of authority. One reason for "centralizing so much power in the office of the Development Administrator is to have it to give back to the people."[1] That is, each community or neighborhood should be permitted to decide planning issues which are proposed for their own areas. As Edward J. Logue, creator and former Director of the BRA says, "'I don't think the people of West Roxbury have any right to decide what goes on in the South End. That is for the people of the South End to decide.'"[2] But Logue does believe that unwise decisions made by the citizens in a particular community should not be supported "unless doing so would jeopardize the entire planning effort."[3] Thus, citizens in Boston are given the opportunity to express their views, but the city retains the authority to override "unwise decisions." Cook sees in the discretionary approach the possibility of abuse by a developer "who takes advantage of a weak market or makes use of political connections to improve his bargaining position." He also says that a city may use discretionary review "to obtain privately financed public improvements."[4]

Regardless of the intent of the BRA, giving this organization large amounts of authority does increase the risk of corruptive behavior on the part of the design reviewers. But since Boston's design review process is on a smaller scale than in larger cities such as New York and San Francisco and therefore not as complex, Boston's city officials may be more willing to give discretionary authority to the BRA. It may be easier to detect corruptive behavior or incorrect design review procedures in Boston than in a larger city such as New York City.

New York's FASD, on the other hand, has a more self-administered, nondiscretionary approach to design review. Recall that the FASD is primarily concerned with functional elements of design. Design review procedures that concentrate on functional elements can more easily specify particular uses of design elements before the preparation of a design proposal. Furthermore, the elements' effect on the overall project composition can be predicted more easily than the effects of architectural details; hence, FASD's nondiscretionary approach may be best suited to achieve its overall aims. In fact, given that the FASD lacks a complete set of "design" issues, the product of the review may not necessarily be a better design, but may indeed be a functional element. This approach is consistent with the FASD's attempt to rationalize the bonus incentive aspects of its guidelines—a discretionary approach may not function properly in combination with the criteria used to award the bonuses. Eliminating opportunities to negotiate design concerns results in eliminating the use of discretion in awarding development bonuses.

Only in the case of Boston was the discretionary approach used with very limited guidelines; generally, the use of discretionary review without guidelines is rare. Moreover, at the other extreme, completely automatic review is just as rare. Even though the FASD was intended to be self-administering in practice, the intent was not realized because developers and their designers were given the right to include certain options in their development plans. In other words, if they decide to include one or more available options in their designs, they must go through a planning review in which the City Planning Commission has discretion to grant or deny requests for special permits. This planning review is a very long, drawn-out process which can frustrate developers and their designers as well as dramatically increase their front-end costs. The FASD's semi-self-administering approach uses uniform controls to counteract the lack of discretion; but often guidelines such as these tend to be overly restrictive and may "focus on reducing damage, rather than on producing positive results."[5] While there are problems with both of these extreme approaches, in many cases an automatic review cannot adequately be substituted for a discretionary approach, nor can a discretionary approach be an effective substitute for an automatic review.

Minneapolis and San Francisco have adopted a semi-discretionary approach to control design reviews. That is, they selected approaches which have basic characteristics of both the discretionary and self-administering approaches. Minneapolis, for example, reviews each project individually to determine if the proposed development complies with the city zoning ordinance. The ordinance itself is flexible, and the urban designers of the Planning and Development Department have only limited discretion to alter the ordinance. The fact that Minneapolis promotes communication between the public and private sectors of the city reduces the probability of misunderstandings and consequently reduces the amount of pressure the reviewers may need to exert on developers to submit plans which are consistent with Minneapolis's urban design objectives.

Thus, the success of urban design in Minneapolis depends on the degree of communication between the public and private sectors, as well as on the coordination of their efforts. This cooperation and communication has resulted in Minneapolis's encouraging developers and their architects to meet with the urban designers of the Planning and Development Department for numerous informal preliminary design review sessions. The atmosphere of the design review is very informal and relaxed, thereby increasing the chances of the two parties' developing a good working relationship. Furthermore, urban designers working with the developers and their architects are technical experts in urban design and can offer the developer and architects sound advice. The recommendations of the urban designers and planners of the Planning and Development Department carry a great deal of weight with the City Planning Commission, and the influence that this professional staff has on design review outcomes ensures that appropriate and well designed projects will be developed. In Minneapolis, and particularly in the Concept Plan Review, developers accept a great deal of technical input from the urban designers. Although this approach has been relatively successful in the past, problems could occur in the future if government officials do not continue to have the same magnitude of support and dedication as present officials have toward urban design.

San Francisco also uses a semidiscretionary approach to urban design. As in Minneapolis, San Francisco's urban designers serve in an advisory role during the design review sessions, and their recommendations are highly respected by the City Planning Commission. The City Planning Commission in San Francisco has discretionary authority to ensure that urban developments meet the city's objectives; however, many planning decisions are made outside of the Department of City Planning. For instance, "planning responsibilities are held by the Redevelopment Agency; the Mayor's Office of Economic and Community Development; the Art Commission, . . . the Bay Conservation and Development Commission and the California Coastal Commission."[6] Dividing the planning function into so many jurisdictions can reduce the Department of City Planning's ability to influence the direction of major changes that occur in San Francisco. This is different from Boston's approach which combines planning and implementation into one centralized agency. Furthermore, some feel that San Francisco's Department of City Planning has relatively little input into deciding what projects should be pursued. For example, "since the start of federal revenue sharing in 1972, priorities for the mayor's programs have been determined largely by what sorts of federal grants were forthcoming; secondly, by political and social demands; and not at all by priorities set by the City Planning Director."[7] It is likely that San Francisco's urban design policies are suffering because of the division of powers scattered throughout the government of San Francisco and beyond.

Minneapolis is the only city of the four examined that has formal or mandated design reviews. Legislation in Minneapolis specifically states that residential developments with 10 or more dwelling units must go through design review. Although zoning legislation in Boston, New York, and San Francisco does not mandate design review, or in the case of Boston even mention it, city officials have designed their administrative procedures in such a way almost to guarantee that development plans will undergo design review. In these cases, the design reviews are called informal reviews.

Both New York and San Francisco have initiated a process approach to urban design. This approach is characterized by placing emphasis on government goals, objectives, policies, and standards as a means of influencing private development. San Francisco, for instance, has adopted an overall Urban Design Plan which is used as a framework for the design review, and New York's FASD plan is a legal framework which is fashioned to guide development in that district. Boston and Minneapolis, on the other hand, have attempted to influence private development by means of a project-oriented approach. Boston examines each project individually and prepares design criteria which are applicable only to the specific project under review at the time, whereas Minneapolis's project approach is based on the active communication and cooperation of government planning officials and private citizens.

It should now be clear that many factors can influence the type of approach a city selects to control design review. The nature of a city's decision-making strategies—whether centralized or decentralized—will dictate if a city adopts a discretionary or a self-administering approach or some combination of these two approaches. For example, Boston centralizes authority and gives total discretion to the BRA. Of course, the size of the city may also tend to influence governmental officials to select one approach over another.

Large cities tend to have a number of agencies involved in the development process, other than the Planning Department and Planning Commission, and they therefore have multiple channels that a proposed project must go through in order to be approved. New York and San Francisco, for example, have complex decision-making systems and have adopted more of a process approach to design review with little or no discretion given to the design review body. Legislation replaces urban designers' discretionary authority.

Minneapolis and Boston, however, have demonstrated that for urban design to be an effective force within governmental planning processes, "plans" such as those devised in San Francisco and New York need not be required. Minneapolis, in particular, has found that cultivating cooperation between the government planning officials and private citizens in the design review process is the cornerstone of success with development and redevelopment projects.

However, because an approach is successful in one city does not automatically mean that it will be successful in another city. Nor is there general agreement on the "best" approach. Lindbloom,[8] for example, states that single-family detached housing need not be subject to design review. However, I can say that there seems to be a definite relationship between the likelihood for success of urban design review and the "health" of planning and the presence of a master plan, zoning, etc. The nature of the overall city zoning regulations, level of design details to be reviewed, and the availability of resources are additional issues which must be considered when establishing a city's decision-making process. Furthermore, the dynamics of the city must be considered—cities with rapid and diverse development must have a flexible approach applicable to a variety of project designs. A discretionary approach may be best suited in this case. Boston has devised a flexible approach, for example, by placing discretion with the BRA rather than having legislatively determined standards. New York's FASD, on the other hand, has little flexibility—in part, however, to retain control over the bonus system that is incorporated into their guidelines. In conclusion, only after careful deliberation of economic, social, and political characteristics should a city decide on an urban design approach to adopt (see Chapter 13).

Nature

The degree or level of detail provided in the design review guidelines varies among the four models (see Fig. 7-2). Boston has no design guidelines and instead establishes individual guidelines for each development. In this way, the BRA has design guidelines which are tailored to the specific development and at the same time can incorporate aspects of designs which have been successful for previous projects. Thus, Boston can continuously improve the quality of its design review guidelines by including effective guidelines that have been "tested" in the past. The latest design techniques can also be easily incorporated in the guidelines. The lack of prescribed standards, however, can result in a number of problems.

For example, the reviewer and the developer's architect may disagree on some aspects of the proposed design during the design review, but the reviewer has no standards which have been accepted as legitimate to back up his position. The reviewer must rely solely on discretionary authority; consequently, he/she risks jeopardizing congenial working relations with the architect. Furthermore, reviewers working on a specific project may not be in total agreement about the design objectives of the project. Lack of consensus among reviewers would be detrimental to the success of the design review and, therefore, to the proposed project's design.

On the other hand, prescriptive standards that are overly strict and poorly prepared may result in consequences similar to the problems which may occur when there are no guidelines at all. Aesthetic elements of the design, for instance, may suffer if prescriptive standards inadvertently promote blandness or excessive homogeneity. Likewise, there is a chance that designers may object to complying with rigid prescriptive standards which restrict the amount of creative input that can be included in the

Figure 7-2: Nature of Design Review

CITY		BOSTON	MINNEAPOLIS	NEW YORK	SAN FRANCISCO
NONE	GUIDELINES ESTABLISHED FOR EACH PROJECT	●			
PRESCRIPTIVE GUIDELINES	STATEMENT, TEXT		●	●	●
	ILLUSTRATED BY PROTOTYPES				●
	REFERENCES MADE TO SPECIFIC PROJECTS				●
	COMPONENTS			●	
PERFORMANCE GUIDELINES	SPECIFIC MEASURES GIVEN				●
	REFERENCES TO OTHER STANDARDS				
INCENTIVES	DEVELOPMENT BONUSES			●	●
	TAX PAYMENT MANIPULATIONS	●			
GEOGRAPHIC SCOPE	CITY - WIDE		●		●
	SPECIAL DISTRICTS	●		●	●
DEVELOPMENT SCOPE	SELECTED TYPES OF DEVELOPMENTS		●		
	ALL DEVELOPMENTS	●		●	●
PLACEMENT OF GUIDELINES	GUIDELINES CODIFIED INTO CITY ZONING ORDINANCE		●	●	●
	DESIGN MANUAL, GUIDEBOOK				●
	URBAN DESIGN PLAN				●

design solutions. Even well planned prescriptive standards reduce the design options available to developers and their architects. For example, the FASD's guidelines were prepared after extensive studies were conducted in order to identify the elements which would fulfill the specific needs of the district. The guidelines contain a number of options from which the designer may choose, but the options are limited to those which reflect the predetermined needs of the district.

Generally, developers and their architects will tend to accept prescriptive standards if the specific requirements are supported by comprehensive studies. For example, San Francisco's Urban Design Plan was based on a three-year study conducted by their planning staff. Basing the content of the guidelines on actual studies increased their credibility in the eyes of the developers and their architects.

San Francisco is the only city in this study which illustrates standards by using prototypes. San Francisco was able to avoid the major problem associated with prototypes—designer confusion over which aspects of the design to focus on—by using prototypes to illustrate rather than replace the design review guidelines. Using prototypes in the appropriate manner can demonstrate the overall effect of the design controls very effectively. New York's urban designers do not provide prototypes during their reviews. In practice, however, they may refer developers and their architects to an actual component or part of a building, such as an arcade, that has already been built. This gives the developers and their architects an opportunity actually to see what type of components the urban designers desire, thus enabling them to incorporate the lessons learned from that experience into their own design solutions.

The geographic area within which the design review guidelines apply is city-wide for Minneapolis and both city-wide and special district-oriented for San Francisco. City-wide guidelines have to be general and therefore serve more as a framework; the generality necessitates that the design reviewers supply specific requirements at the design review sessions. Designing the guidelines in this manner guarantees that designers will participate in design review sessions, therefore increasing the chance of providing consistent, city-wide urban design. Contrarily, the BRA has adopted an overall design review system to achieve Boston's urban development objectives but applies it in neighborhood settings rather than city-wide. This approach was chosen in order to retain the distinct character of the various sections within Boston. Furthermore, since the city has so many different land formations, one set of uniform standards for the entire city would not be appropriate. Thus, Boston has a mix of local processes or sets of geographically applied standards which are administered centrally by the BRA. Similarly, the FASD's guidelines apply solely to specific areas of Fifth Avenue.

Design review may be applied to all developments or only to selected types of developments and redevelopments throughout a city. The guidelines for Boston, New York, and San Francisco cover all types of developments, while Minneapolis's guidelines are applicable to residential developments of 10 dwelling units or more.

Since design review is an implemental tool, it is important that the city adopt legislation which enables the review body to take appropriate action. Minneapolis, for example, has devoted a section of its zoning ordinance to design review procedures. The legislation describes the purpose, geographic and development scope, and design review procedures. The Concept Plan Review focuses on the process itself rather than on substantive issues. This is advantageous both to the designer because he or she is more aware of what is expected during the design review process and to the city because the designer is mandated to attend design review sessions. Furthermore, the urban designers will be guaranteed the opportunity to interpret the prescriptive standards which are outlined in the City of Minneapolis Zoning Ordinance.

The FASD's guidelines, as contained in Chapter 7 of the City of New York Zoning Ordinance, clearly outline prescribed design guidelines but do not advise or even inform the developer that he can seek consultation with OMPD. Consequently, the legislation does not mention the advantages of participating in design review. Encouraging developers and architects to seek the advice of OMPD, however, could increase the effectiveness of this special district in a number of ways. First, OMPD has a technical staff which could advise the developers and their architects on how to incorporate all of the regulations and bonuses into their designs. The design review body can explain ambiguous standards and point out how to include the maximum number of public amenities. Since including public amenities in new developments is not mandatory, the design review can serve as a valuable means of motivating developers and architects to include desired amenities. Second, the design review body can support the developers' and architects' requests for special permits and perhaps explain the rationale behind their requests to the CPC. Aside from the influence OMPD may exert on the CPC, design review can also help the developers and architects submit special permits which have a greater chance of being accepted. This would be invaluable to the developer and architect because the planning process alone takes six months, and during this time front-end costs increase substantially.

Consulting with OMPD ultimately benefits the developers and architects, New York City, and the public. Developers and architects benefit if the information provided from the design review helps them get a special permit passed the first time around because they will incur lower front-end costs. Additionally, taking advantage of the incentives and bonuses can increase the revenues from the development substantially. The city can benefit from design sessions in two ways. First, since additional revenues will be generated from mixed use developments on the Avenue, the city may benefit if the design review encourages developers to adopt as many bonuses as possible. Second, if OMPD persuades developers and architects to incorporate desired public amenities into their developments, this demonstrates to the public that the FASD was indeed successful, and the public is likely to be more supportive of future zoning plans which attempt to alleviate other urban development problems in New York City. The public certainly benefits because desired amenities are being provided and the character of Fifth Avenue is being restored.

Boston is the only city which does not have written guidelines. Urban designers consequently do not have specific legislative power, but the discretionary power which they have compensates effectively for the lack of prescribed guidelines. Strong political and public support further enhances the power the BRA has over development in downtown Boston. However, there are disadvantages: developers and their architects tend to be totally unaware of the planning process by which development plans are submitted, reviewed, modified, and presented for approval; and they and the public cannot help being unaware of the criteria used to judge the projects. However, if the BRA design review produces acceptable products over a number of years, the public's trust in the BRA's capabilities will grow. At the same time, the lack of written criteria may be acceptable and in fact desirable to many developers and architects since it gives them an opportunity to prepare creative designs and at least to present and discuss their points of view at the initial design review session.

The FASD's guidelines are somewhat unique because incentives in the form of floor area bonuses are used to encourage developers to adopt plans which are consistent with the district's needs. The FASD's design control focuses on components because bonus awards are more easily allocated using this unit—each amenity element is worth a certain amount in FAR. The effectiveness of incentive zoning, however, remains a controversial issue. Some believe this approach produces desired design results, while others feel that the costs that the city must bear in order to obtain the amenities are higher than the benefits accrued from the amenities. In fact, developers may receive more financial benefits by taking advantage of the bonus system than the city receives.

Furthermore, there is no mechanism in the FASD guidelines to ensure that the public amenities developers say they will include in their designs will actually be provided. For instance, developers may agree to build terraces or provide a galleria on the ground floor of their buildings, but there is no insurance that these public amenities will be completed in a satisfactory manner. The landscape on the terrace may simply consist of a few bushes and trees scattered around haphazardly, and the galleria may never be finished. Compounding the negative consequences of zoning by incentives is the lack of penalties for not supplying the amenities which were agreed upon during the design review. The reviewers have no recourse if the designers choose to alter characteristics of the amenities. Boston also has an incentive mechanism. A special tax provision gives the BRA authority to negotiate real estate tax payment. While this benefits the developer because the tax rate is fixed and often lower than conventional methods of tax assessment, the city benefits because the developer must go through design review sessions before the BRA will grant the developer the special tax break. Thus, the BRA can direct development in Boston where it is most desired.

The factors which determine the nature of design review are

related to the degree of detail found in the design review guidelines. Yet, the guidelines' detail depends on the characteristics of the elements being controlled and the degree of control which the city wishes to maintain. For example, the city of Boston wants its urban designers and planners to have total authority over all urban renewal projects in downtown Boston. The discretionary judgment of the urban designers and planners has been substituted for written prescribed guidelines in order for the city to retain the type of control it desires. New York, on the other hand, has geographic and development scopes similar to those in Boston; but instead of giving urban designers discretionary power, the city has codified prescriptive guidelines into the City Zoning Ordinance. Apparently city officials in New York feel they can maintain the level of control over development on Fifth Avenue more effectively by restricting the role of their urban designers to one which is advisory in nature, thereby placing authority, and thus control, in city legislation. Hence, the nature of design review guidelines is determined to a large degree by the intent of the guidelines but more importantly by the control methods or mechanisms that the city selects. That is, authority may be granted to the urban designers, as in Boston, to the review ordinance, as in New York, or the power may be distributed among both the urban designers and review ordinance, as in San Francisco and Minneapolis.

Elements

Developers, architects, and reviewers tend to be most concerned with the elements of the guidelines—the components of a proposed design which are controlled by the design review guidelines. The final product will be determined mainly by the type of elements contained in the guidelines, and therefore the elements may be the source of design disputes between the architect and the reviewer.

Figure 7-3 lists issues which are used to compare the elements of

Figure 7-3: Elements of Design Review

SAN FRANCISCO	NEW YORK	MINNEAPOLIS	BOSTON	CITY	
●	●	●	●	LOCATION	COMPATIBILITY
●	●	●	●	LAND USE	
●	●	●	●	HEIGHT, BULK, F.A.R.	
●	●	●	●	STREETLINE, SETBACK	
●	●	●	●	COVERAGE	
●	●	●	●	ACCESS, PARKING, LOADING, SERVICE	EXTERNAL EFFECTS
●		●	●	LANDSCAPING, PAVING, SIGNS	
●	●	●	●	AMENITIES, RECREATION	
				SURVEILLANCE	
●				SCENIC EASEMENT	
●		●	●	SCALE, STYLES	ARCHITECTURAL ISSUES
●				ROOF - CORNICE	
●				AWNING, PORCH, PROJECTION	
●			●	ARCADES, STAIRS	
●				MATERIAL, COLOR, TEXTURE	
				FACADE DETAILS	

the four design review procedures. These issues do not have a direct ordinal ranking, although the scale or scope of the items does narrow further down the list. In other words, items 1 through 5 deal with massing and siting concerns, items 6 through 10 include external effects of projects, and items 11 through 16 relate to architectural detailing issues. The description of the design review models illustrates that each city's procedures include a different range of issues and places emphasis on different portions of the 16 control issues. Figure 7-3 compares the four models against the list of 16 issues in order to identify their primary focus and shows that models which emphasize functional issues tend to focus more on siting and massing elements. The four models examined in this study are similar in one respect—they are all concerned with functional concerns; however, the degree that they are concerned with aesthetic issues varies among the models.

The FASD guidelines deal exclusively with functional concerns and focus primarily on siting and massing—provision of public amenities and access, parking, and loading issues—but address no architectural detailing issues at all. One major problem with the FASD's guidelines is that the regulations do not mention the importance of coordinating old and new buildings on the Avenue. Thus, buildings which are drastically different from present structures in height and appearance may be constructed. This lack of integration has corroded the district's character further as buildings "much too big and too bulky for traditional, gracious Fifth Avenue" have begun to be built.[9] Neglecting to include compatibility concerns in the guidelines does not support the major purpose of creating the FASD—to retain the distinct character of Fifth Avenue—and is a serious omission.

Boston, Minneapolis, and San Francisco focus, in varying degrees, on aesthetic concerns. For instance, Minneapolis's primary concern is to "insure a satisfactory relationship of the proposed development with the site" and to ensure that the new development is "compatible with the character of the surrounding neighborhood."[10] Thus, architectural issues of scale and style are important elements in Minneapolis's guidelines. Similarly, Boston and San Francisco are also concerned with compatibility of their developments and redevelopments; however, San Francisco's guidelines are more comprehensive than Boston's because San Francisco includes elements dealing with roofing and cornice, and awning, porches, and projections.

None of the examined models except that of San Francisco focused on very detailed architectural concerns—materials used in the building, window size, or wall details—or on interior design elements such as apartment unit layout. The patterns which appear to evolve from the four models examined in this study do not imply that all design guidelines of similar slant will adopt the same patterns of concerns. But the purpose or objective of the design review process will dictate the content of the controls incorporated in the design review guidelines. However, the 16 elements in Figure 7-3 present a "reasonable" and "practical" list of elements to be covered in guidelines.

Management

Proper management of design review can greatly enhance the successes and accomplishments of the design review process. Critical aspects of the administrative process are the amount of time it takes, adequate staffing, and financial resources. For instance, bureaucratic red tape that is often associated with urban design reviews consumes much of the developer's time and money and can be a source of frustration. San Francisco's administrative procedure, for example, takes a minimum of 24 weeks from the time the developer submits a set of preliminary plans until he receives a decision on his project. Similarly, New York's administrative process takes a minimum of 20 weeks.

In comparison, Minneapolis's Concept Plan Review is more time conscious and accelerates the process considerably. After a developer submits his initial concept plans, a neighborhood meeting must be scheduled within two weeks. The time span between the neighborhood meeting, the public hearing, and the city council's final vote is a maximum of 60 days, unless there is a developer's delay. Since the city council has only 30 days from the public hearing to make a decision, a developer can calculate in advance the latest possible date he will receive a decision about his project. He will then be able to know his front-end costs much earlier and consequently make more efficient financial arrange-

ments. Boston's administrative process is slightly faster than
Minneapolis, approximately eight weeks. Recall, however, that
Minneapolis requires a neighborhood meeting be scheduled for
each proposed development. The two-week discrepancy between
Minneapolis's and Boston's administrative process is due to this
mandated neighborhood meeting.

There are a number of reasons that San Francisco and New York
require 24 weeks and 20 weeks respectively to decide on a project's
acceptability. First, the size of the bureaucracy is directly related to
the size of the city. It stands to reason that New York or San
Francisco would have a larger bureaucracy than Minneapolis or
Boston and therefore require more time because more people have
to be consulted during the process. Also related to the size of the
city is the number of projects reviewed each year. The more
projects a city must review will result in people having to wait in
line for their projects to be reviewed. Additionally, public hearings
will be harder to schedule.

Resources are another important component of the administrative process—a city needs sufficient funds in order to operate its
agencies efficiently. However, there is evidence that some cities are
beginning to feel a financial crunch. For instance, San Francisco's
Department of City Planning experienced a budget cut due to
Jarvis-Gann's Proposition 13 and subsequently was forced to merge
the urban design staff with the permit process staff in fiscal year
1979–80.[11] Currently, the city's planning function has a budget "just
over $1 million—slightly less than during Jacobs's regime" as
Director of the City Planning Department from 1967 through
1974.[12] Charles Gill of San Francisco's Department of City Planning
feels that the quality of the department's work has been
substantially affected since the budget reductions took place.[13] This
is to be expected, since the merger reduced the amount of time the
urban designers can devote to advising developers and their
architects on urban design issues. Thus, the quality of design
reviews could be affected dramatically with the budget cut since
approximately 500 applications for new developments are approved in San Francisco each year and an additional 2,000
applications are submitted for redevelopment permits.[14]

New York is also experiencing substantial financial problems. In
fact quite recently OMPD has been merged with the Manhattan
Office.[15] This move has occurred primarily because of enormous

financial difficulties that the city is currently experiencing. One of the major problems is that federal aid is being cut and will continue to be cut even more in the future. The city is also trying to increase the efficiency of its operation by coordinating the different units and the professional expertise that has previously been spread throughout Manhattan. They hope centralizing the operation in one location will increase effectiveness.[16]

Minneapolis and Boston do not have the financial problems that San Francisco and New York are experiencing. In fact, John Burg of Minneapolis's Planning Department has stated that city resources are sufficiently high and that the city has no problem in regards to money.[17] Boston, too, has few money problems currently, although its money supply is moderate and becoming tighter over time.

Boston, however, is somewhat different from the other cities examined in this study in that the BRA is not technically a city agency. Rather, the BRA, as a redevelopment authority created by the legislature, is considered a state agency and is responsible to a board comprised of five members—one member appointed by the Governor of Massachusetts and the other four appointed by the Mayor of Boston. These board members are private citizens and meet biweekly. In contrast to the other three cities, most of the BRA's operating funds came from HUD (now HHS) and only a small portion comes from the city. Therefore, Boston is better off from a financial perspective than the other cities which must rely on receiving operating money solely from the cities themselves.

An effective design review process depends on the staff which administers it. The number of urban designers assigned to design review in New York, for example, varies according to the complexity of the project (see Fig. 7-4). If a developer and his architect simply need advice, the Director and/or Deputy Director will be involved in the review. But when projects are actually reviewed and recommendations are to be submitted to the CPC the design review staff increases: two to three urban designers are assigned to the review, plus one or two planners and two other commission members who are experts in economic and transportation issues. Thus, the number of personnel assigned to a particular review varies depending on the size and nature of the project. Generally, two to six staff members will review projects; and out of this total, one to three individuals will be urban designers.

Minneapolis's staff is somewhat smaller than New York's, with a

CITY	STAFFING					TIME	CITY RESOURCES		
	SPECIAL DESIGN REVIEW BOARD	PLANNING DEPARTMENT	PLANNING COMMISSION	NUMBER OF URBAN DESIGNERS	NUMBER OF OTHER MEMBERS	MINIMUM TIME REQUIREMENT	HIGH	MODERATE	LOW
BOSTON	●			1-2	4-5	8 wks		●	
MINNEAPOLIS		●	●	1	2	10 wks	●		
NEW YORK	●		●	1-3	1-5	20 wks			●
SAN FRANCISCO		●	●	1-3	1-3	24 wks			●

Figure 7-4: Management of Design Review

total of five urban designers in the entire Department of Planning and Development. In every Concept Plan Review, there are three personnel working on a proposed design: one urban designer, one community planner, and the Zoning Administrator from the Building Department.

Boston usually assigns five to six reviewers to each project—one urban designer, a planner, a member from a legal association, and two other members of the BRA who are economic and transportation experts. The Director of Urban Design may also become involved in the review if the size and nature of the project warrants it. A total of eleven urban designers work for the BRA, and one urban designer is assigned to a particular project and is involved with that project throughout the complete review process.

Thus, the number of personnel assigned to design reviews varies from city to city. As financial resources become more scarce, the size of design review staffs will likely decrease. The number of urban designers and planners in New York, for instance, has diminished because of the financial problems the city is experiencing. This situation may continue to worsen throughout the country. Recall that San Francisco's design review staff has taken on the responsibility of reviewing permit applications in addition to their review duties. Even though the number of personnel may not have been reduced numerically, in reality this translates into a decrease in personnel since the urban design staff no longer devotes most of their time to design review.

San Francisco's problems have been further compounded by the overlaps between the design process and the environmental review. As stated previously, San Francisco's discretionary review process includes three separate reviews—a planning review, environmental review, and design review.[18] These overlaps may result in unnecessary costs and delays for the developer and his architect and may reduce the volume of projects the urban design staff can review. Coordination and simplification of these processes can enhance the ability of the design review process to produce more effective and successful urban developments in San Francisco.

San Francisco is the only city examined in this study which is mandated to prepare environmental reviews. Minneapolis does require that an "Environmental Worksheet" be submitted for every project proposed to be built within the city. But this worksheet is a very straightforward questionnaire that is used to determine whether or not an Environmental Impact Report is needed. The size and nature of the project are other factors which also influence Minneapolis's decision to require an Environmental Impact Report. New York and Minneapolis do not automatically require Environmental Impact Reports; however, depending on the size and nature of the project, New York may require developers to submit such a report.

In Boston, the Massachusetts Environmental Policy Act (MEPA) requires "the review and evaluation of projects to describe their environmental impacts and establishes a process for determining when Environmental Impact Reports are required."[19] In general, urban renewal projects are exempt from environmental reviews "since the renewal plans either pre-dated MEPA or did undergo environmental review as a function of planning approval."[20] Urban renewal activities which are funded from Boston's urban renewal budget do not require the BRA to conduct environmental reviews; rather, HUD must conduct the reviews. The National Environmental Policy Act requires Environmental Impact Assessments

(EIA) for any project undertaken by a federal agency or requiring federal approval or financial assistance. Federal agencies may, however, establish their own procedures.[21] Private projects which require a BRA permit or financial assistance must have an environmental review conducted by the BRA unless the project is categorically excluded. For example, projects are exempt if the proposed development contains fewer than 100 residential units or is a nonresidential development that costs less than $500,000.

Our comparative study of the models presented in this chapter identifies numerous common themes as well as the discrepancies among the four models. The crucial factors are the applicability and the responsiveness of a design review process. This relationship of the models to their specific environments remains to be assessed in the next chapters and will be revealed through analysis of case studies.

Notes

1. Langley C. Keynes, Jr. (1969). *The Rehabilitation Planning Game: A Study in the Diversity of Neighborhood* (Cambridge, Mass.: MIT Press), p. 30.

2. *Ibid.*

3. *Ibid.*

4. Robert S. Cook, Jr. (1980). *Zoning for Downtown Urban Design* (Lexington, Mass.: Lexington Books), p. 157.

5. Weiming Lu (1977). "Successful Urban Design in Local Government," *Practicing Planner,* 7:32.

6. Gerald D. Adams (1980). "San Francisco: Utopia Reconsidered," *Planning,* 46:16.

7. *Ibid.*

8. Carl E. Lindbloom (1970). *Environmental Design Review.* (West Trenton, N.J.: Chandler Davis Publishing), p. 12.

9. News Report, "Retail Construction: Wholesale Destruction" (1979). *Progressive Architecture,* 60:25.

10. *City of Minneapolis Zoning Ordinance* (1976). Concept Plan Review, Section 534.450, (1), p. 3778.

11. San Francisco Department of City Planning (1979). *Annual Report, 1978–79,* p. 28.

12. Adams (1980), p. 16.

13. Charles Gill (1980). Personal conversation, March 24.

14. San Francisco Department of City Planning (1975). *Memorandum* to the City Planning Commission from Dean L. Macris, Director of Planning, March 13, p. 2.

15. Glenn Fowler (1980). "Planning Agency Breaks up Urban Design Group," *The New York Times*, March 28: Section A, p. 26.

16. Lauren Otis (1980). Personal conversation, March 24.

17. John Burg (1980). Personal conversation, March 24.

18. San Francisco Department of City Planning (1975), p. 9.

19. Massachusetts Office of Environmental Affairs (1979). *Memorandum* from Richard Mertens to staff, Environmental Review Officers, September 24, p. 1.

20. *Ibid.*

21. *Ibid.*, pp. 1–3.

22. *Ibid.*, pp. 4–5.

Part III

The Case Studies

8
General Introduction to the Case Studies

Design review can take place in a wide variety of environments or situations. This section of the volume examines four design review processes that have taken place in Boston, Minneapolis, New York, and San Francisco. Case studies such as these are used to isolate a part of the complex world; they provide a rich source of data and an opportunity for insight offered in real world situations. Although each case is unique, the case studies can be related to a larger environmental framework; and inferences can be drawn from the cases which explain to some degree how to apply different design review models to different environments. Thus, the cases provide data and the basis for making generalizations.

The four cases examined are The Charlestown Savings Bank, Boston; The Crossing, Minneapolis; Olympic Tower, New York; and One Market Plaza, San Francisco. These cases are selected from a wide variety of situations—different geographical, political, sociocultural, legal, and managerial environments. For instance, San Francisco's topography of hills and scenic views is quite different from the downtown areas of New York City, Boston, and Minneapolis; Boston's historical preservation emphasis is unlike Minneapolis's predominantly functional approach to urban design. Furthermore, San Francisco and New York City have larger bureaucracies than either Boston or Minneapolis; and while New York City's political system is undoubtedly more complex and cumbersome than San Francisco's, these two cities have adopted urban design reviews with varying degrees of discretionary power left in the hands of the planning personnel.

Examining the day-to-day activities of design review in the cities of Boston, Minneapolis, New York City, and San Francisco will, however, provide firsthand knowledge of real world occurrences. Thus, case information will provide the basis for some general "observations." These observations are not applicable to all design review settings, but rather they are applicable to situations which are similar in some respects to the cases studied here. Hence, the lessons learned in these four cities on design review may not be all applicable to other cities; some of the lessons are quite applicable to all cities. The lessons are particularly useful for other cities which plan to institute a design review mechanism.

We shall examine each case study along three separate lines: background setting, design review process, and analysis and observations. Background setting describes the location, function, and components of each building, its significance, the main design issues surrounding this building, and laws and regulations applicable to each building's design. The architectural firm, construction firm, developer, and consulting firms associated with a specific case study are also listed.

Discussion of the design review process will include information on the members of the design review team and the length of the design review process for each case. A detailed description of the design review process will then be examined; finally, various critiques of the resultant product will be presented.

Under analysis and observations we shall examine specific responses of the reviewers and reviewees during the design review and the reasons these actors made particular responses and decisions in each case. For example, political, social, and economical pressure may have influenced decisions of the actors.

The following additional issues will also be discussed in this section:

- Whether the reviewers and reviewees acted on behalf of the public.
- If the building examined in the case study was successful.
- If the design review process served a useful and effective purpose.
- Positive and negative aspects of the design review.
- Whether external power modified any of the decisions made by either the reviewers or reviewees.
- How effectively the urban designers played their roles.

An individual case study may not include all of the above issues;

thus, each time we shall address only those points which are relevant to that specific case study.

We will then be ready in the last section of the book to reexamine and compare cases and prepare a list of general observations derived from the characteristics of each case study (Chapter 13). We shall further analyze and expand our observations in order to identify specific environmental factors which have played a significant role in influencing each city's use of a specific procedure. The environmental factors also will be used in Chapter 14 to relate particular aspects of the design review models to the particular environmental setting.

9
Boston:
Charlestown Savings Bank

The Charlestown Savings Bank building, situated in Boston's central business district, is located at the corner of Summer and Chauncy Streets (see Figs. 9-1 to 9-5). This section of Summer Street is dominated by Jordan Marsh and Filenes, two of Boston's largest department stores. The site of the Charlestown Savings Bank is one block from Washington Street, a traffic-free pedestrian mall. The buildings on Washington Street are predominantly retail at the ground floor and contain a combination of retail and office space at the upper levels. Chauncy Street will penetrate the center of Lafayette Place, a major retail, office, hotel, entertainment, and parking complex that has been proposed several blocks south of Summer Street. Additional traffic demands are placed on Chauncy Street because traffic on Washington Street has been closed off.

To handle the projected traffic load, the Boston Redevelopment Authority (BRA) has realigned Chauncy Street with Arch Street so that traffic feeds across Summer Street. By doing this, the section of Summer Street that extends from Washington Street to the Chauncy-Arch alignment has also been closed to traffic. Thus, the pedestrian mall was extended to the front of Charlestown Savings Bank (see Fig. 9-5). The client of this project was the Charlestown Savings Bank, and The Architects Collaborative (TAC) was the architectural firm selected to design the building. The Vappi Construction Company was responsible for general construction.

BRA's design policy in the Shopping District is intended to encourage developers to provide small vest-pocket mini-parks and other pedestrian amenities to relieve some of the congestion of the area's narrow sidewalks. No formally adopted comprehensive plan for this open space exists, but developers are generally aware of the city's downtown pedestrian policy.

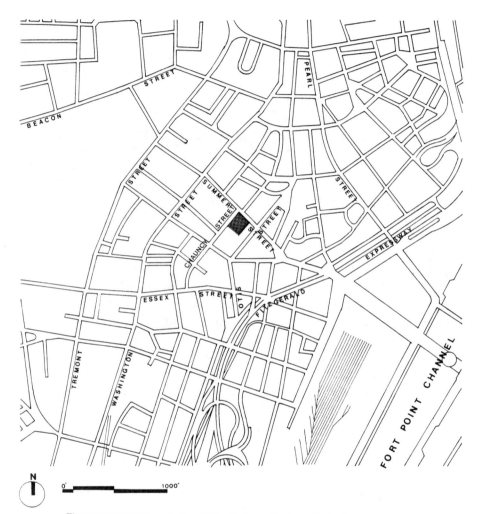

Figure 9-1: Location of site of Charlestown Savings Bank, Boston

The design controls for Charlestown Savings Bank were quite broad: there were no specific written design guidelines for the site, but general requirements were stipulated in Boston's zoning ordinance. As previously discussed, these general requirements deal with issues of siting, massing, and compatibility. The zoning regulations in Boston usually make it necessary for developers to apply for some sort of variance or special exception. Since the proposed floor area density of the Charlestown Savings Bank was less than the zoned maximum of 10 FAR, it did not require a

Figure 9-2: View of Charlestown Savings Bank from Sumner and Chauncy Streets

Figure 9-3: Closer view of Charlestown Savings Bank

Figure 9-4: View of Charlestown Savings Bank along Sumner Street showing Jordan March on the right

Figure 9-5: View of Sumner Street Mall extending pedestrian movement to Charlestown Savings Bank

zoning variance for density. However, its design plan did include parking, which constitutes a conditional use, and there were also several other minor variances needed before a building permit could be granted. In addition, the Chauncy-Arch realignment called for negotiations between the BRA and the bank. Thus, the project was subject to design review.

The design review procedure for the Charlestown Savings Bank was discretionary and entirely in the control of the BRA urban design staff. Since many design issues are already controlled by zoning regulations, the objective of this design review is to examine closely all details of the buildings to ensure that the public's needs and desires will be fulfilled. The BRA's urban designers and the project's developer and architect discuss design criteria that are appropriate for the particular project under review.

Since the developer of the Charlestown Savings Bank applied for a Chapter 121A tax exemption, the project became subject to BRA design review, a public hearing, and BRA Board approval before the application was submitted to the mayor for final approval. Thus design review now was required for two reasons.

Richard Josline, Urban Design Director of BRA, and John Sloan, Urban Designer for BRA, were both directly involved in the design review of Charlestown Savings Bank. Other individuals associated with the design review were Fred Garvin, Boston Public Works Department and a representative of the Charlestown Savings Bank. The following members of TAC were involved in this project: John C. Harkness, principal; Richard Puffer, Associate and Architect-in-Charge; Robert Swain, Architect; Design Team; and Larry Zuelke; Head of the Landscape Department.

The Charlestown Savings Bank's design review process began very well; within a few months Josline, Sloan, Puffer, Swain, and Zuelke had agreed on the basic design of the building. When TAC started to prepare the preliminary working drawings, Puffer became more active in the review process than he had been during the first few months of the design review.

Swain had worked on the layout of the Charlestown Savings Bank's plaza. After considerable work and many design review meetings, an acceptable design solution was found. Eighteen trees were to be arranged in an informal but carefully planned pattern. The tree trunks would rise directly from the ground with only small patches of soil interrupting the brick paving pattern. Sloan thought the design was good and was quite satisfied with the results of the review process.[1]

In September 1974, Charlestown Savings Bank decided to apply for 121A tax benefits for its office building project. Developers often apply for these 121A tax agreements after the planning for their project has started. Perhaps their original plans prove to be less profitable than anticipated; at this later stage, the developer decides it might be better to try to substitute the tax savings possible under 121A for higher profits. The 121A agreement required the Bank to furnish another set of plans with the 121A forms.

Upon examination of this second set of plans submitted in early October, Sloan and Josline found them to be different than the original set. Did changes in the plaza come because of the bank's monetary concerns? Puffer's first schematic design was acceptable to the BRA, but it was expensive for the client. Sloan felt that client pressure may have influenced Puffer's decision to alter the original design.[2]

In mid-October, Sloan requested another set of plaza plans, and he was surprised to find that these plans retained the same omissions as the second set of plans. In a memorandum to BRA's Joe Berlandi, Sloan wrote,

> the previous design has been eliminated and in its place a watered-down version has taken form. The proposed revision of this park leaves almost everything to be desired considering the far superior plan that came before as well as our urban design criteria for that area.[3]

Sloan felt that the September plan

> was consistent with our understanding at that time that this design would enhance work we are doing in the area on pedestrian movement as well as creating a highly attractive and positive urban space on Summer Street.[4]

He was further concerned that the plaza was no longer viable; the landscaping buffer between the loading dock and parking area and the sidewalk along Kingston Street also had been entirely removed.[5] It was Sloan's estimate that these deletions would decrease the cost of this $9.3 million development by approximately $6,000.

TAC's new plan called for trees individually set in raised

planters,[6] rather than trees planted in wells covered with grating (see Figs. 9-6 and 9-7). Sloan and Josline recalled previous plantings in downtown plazas, and Sloan stated that TAC's proposal "did not look urban" and broke with Boston tradition. They further thought that people should be able to walk throughout the plaza area without dodging planters, and they were convinced that the original design was far superior. Puffer expressed his concern, shared with Swain, that the trees would do better if they were set above possible salt damage. Likewise, said Puffer, maintenance of the plaza and the trees would be easier.[7]

Sloan strongly felt that the tax advantages should be given only to a project of superior design. He felt the September design was superior and that there could be no compromise which would jeopardize the public's use and enjoyment of the plaza.[8]

Later design reviews attended by Sloan, Josline, Puffer, Swain, and by representatives of the bank and the Vappi Construction Company revealed this landscape issue as the only stumbling block to plan approval. Puffer held firm. During one of the design review sessions a bank representative finally admitted that the revised plans were intended to cut costs. Arguments continued, and some personal animosities emerged. Sloan wondered if Puffer's design arguments were not rhetorical, while Puffer maintained that the BRA was attempting to impose standards that were subjective rather than empirical.[9] At this point, negotiation became extremely difficult.

According to Sloan, TAC's landscape department preferred the original design and asked his support for it. Was Sloan also looking for Puffer to play the "architect's game" in these sessions? That is, did Sloan want Puffer to make a deal to appear to fight for his client's position while actually intending to yield to demands for the "superior design?"[10] The arguments continued for two months.

Meanwhile, a representative of the bank contacted the BRA Director and requested that Sloan's position on the planter controversy be overruled. This request was denied; since the impasse persisted, Sloan decided to take the initiative. Sloan contacted TAC's Harkness and asked him to restrain Puffer. Eventually, Puffer admitted that Harkness did in fact prefer the original design without planters; two other members of TAC, Swain and Zuelke, also preferred it. The issue was resolved in March. Only two zoning code violations remained to be resolved,

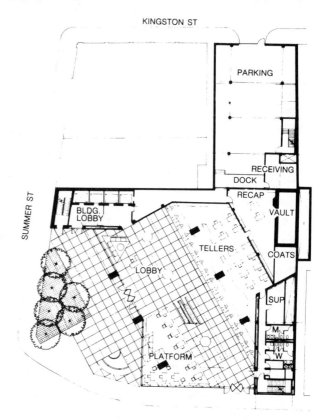

KINGSTON ST

PARKING

RECEIVING
DOCK

RECAP

VAULT

BLDG.
LOBBY

SUMMER ST

TELLERS

COATS

LOBBY

SUP

M

PLATFORM

W

Figure 9-6: Plaza, Charlestown Bank. TAC's original
design scheme with raised
planters

CHAUNCY ST

GROUND FLOOR

∠ N

20′
6m

Figure 9-7: View of Charlestown Savings Bank plaza as built

Figure 9-8: View of Charlestown Savings Bank plaza with seating and in-set trees

Figure 9-9: Facade of Charlestown Savings Bank at ground level in relation to plaza

the parapet setback and the surface parking lot. A Sloan memorandum in early March, 1975 recommended granting a variance for the first problem and accepting the second, although it was subject to compliance with drawings submitted for approval in December, 1974.[11]

Next came the public hearing on the project. Before the meeting, a member of the BRA Board questioned whether the site could accurately be designated as blighted, a stipulation contained in the 121A legislation.[12] During the meeting, some protest over the tax deal was voiced, but there was no apparent concern about design issues.

The abutters did not appear at the hearing and were apparently unconcerned, but they did not speak in favor of the amenities, either. Indeed, there is no strong downtown constituency concerned with design. No one had enough at stake to support more open space in exchange for built-in tax subsidies. There were, however, many people who opposed, in principle, any type of subsidy for commercial buildings.

It took one and a half years for the Charlestown Savings Bank to go through the planning and design review processes and receive a building permit. Construction of the bank proceeded according to the agreed-upon plan, and in March, 1977, the new Charlestown Savings Bank Headquarters was officially opened. The 18 honey locust trees set at grade have done well. Today, the trees have grown beautifully, and the plaza acts as an active and interesting component of Boston's downtown urban plan (see Figs. 9-8 and 9-9).

In April, 1977, Robert Campbell, a journalist for the *Boston Sunday Globe*, praised the bank as "a welcome example of good urban design"[13] (see Fig. 9-10). He felt that it blended well with the neighboring buildings and that the design successfully turned the corner from Chauncy to Summer. The plaza served as an active forecourt for people-watching, and its openness extended visually into the banking floor beyond. Overall, this critic was impressed with the design of the structure and the plaza for the contribution they made to the downtown amenities.

BRA's Sloan was able to retain control and win his point of view largely because the design required his approval before construction could begin. While he was fortunate to have support from Josline and executive support from higher levels of the BRA, it is

Figure 9-10: Charlestown
Savings Bank, overall view

unlikely that the "planters" issue was serious enough for the BRA
Director or the mayor to risk straining administrative relationships.
During the design review process, Sloan moved beyond the review
members and directly appealed to TAC's Harkness on the
professional grounds of good design. Whether or not this action
actually affected the final outcome or even the duration of the
duration of the impasses is uncertain, but it does illustrate one
route of influence that Sloan had at his disposal.

Puffer, on the other hand, had only two available options to try
to convince Sloan, Josline, and the rest of the BRA staff of the value
of his design. First, he argued his point of view; and second, he
presented "expert technical opinion" on the effect of salt on trees.
These tactics, however, could not effectively counteract the
authority of the need for Sloan's final approval.

Even the bank officials were relatively impotent in this case.
They could not support every developer's ultimate threat: to walk
away from the project and let the deal fall through for the city. The

dollars saved with Puffer's revised design simply did not warrant their risking 121A status or squandering the effort expended in preparing their project. Their final attempt to override Sloan may have been merely a gesture to save face; no matter what strategy Puffer or the bank tried to employ, Sloan's authority remained uncontestable.

Both TAC and the BRA Urban Design Staff espoused commitment to design quality. It is generally conceded that Charlestown Savings Bank's design does measure up to TAC's high standards of quality. All along TAC maintained a commitment to an abstract ideal of design quality based on user satisfaction, while Sloan and the BRA remained committed to their interpretation of design quality as embodied in a broad overall policy on pedestrian amenities. Sloan's appeal to Harkness—his going to the head of TAC—brought the issue to a head. Harkness yielded to the necessity of maintaining good relationships with BRA. TAC eventually followed the BRA concept of "good design," even though there was no clear consensus on exactly which proposal really was "better" urban design. TAC chose to yield to Sloan's opinion rather than drag out the conflict of professional opinions: economics proved more powerful than "good" urban design.

However, differences in professional opinions may not have been the only factor which affected the progress of the design review process. According to Puffer, TAC looked for design criteria applicable to the bank project, but found only those of John Sloan.[14] Should TAC have been expected to accept BRA design criteria that were not spelled out, written, and well established in advance? Such a situation left the door open for differences of opinion on "good design."

There was also a difference in professional opinion over what constitutes a good design review process. Puffer was the architect most directly involved in the Charlestown Savings Bank controversy at TAC, and his feelings about the design review process in this particular case are quite positive. Puffer does question Sloan's use of the power of his position to obtain his "personal opinion" of good design. While Puffer believes design review is quite necessary, he feels it can be a counterproductive process when it is extended to control design details rather than applied to issues of form and massing. The details, he contends, ought to be left to the architect who is more aware of the particulars of the situation. He questions whether design review contributed to the quality of the Charlestown Savings Bank design.[15] Overall, however, Puffer feels that Charlestown Savings Bank design is very successful, even without the planters.

Sloan's approach is more functional than Puffer's. He says that the mark of good urban design is the service it brings to direct users and the public. Meeting users' needs is more important than the acclaim of the architect's peers. The success of a design review process depends on the end product's compatibility, its user impacts, its future state, and its offerings to the public. Sloan agrees that the Charlestown Savings Bank design is good, but he feels that the review process was exceedingly long and difficult.[16]

The powers that the BRA exercises on 121A applications and zoning conditional uses are based on police powers of the state—a much less definitive form of control than ownership. However, if a developer seeks 121A tax benefits, he should expect to pay the price of more controls over his project.

In addition, Puffer's challenge of Sloan's authority to work from discretionary criteria might have been avoided if the criteria had been available earlier. In fact, some of the problems that occurred at the design review might have been avoided if the BRA had provided written guidelines for the developer and his architects to follow—or at least provided the criteria used for Boston's urban design policies in writing. Written criteria which reflected Sloan's views would have made Sloan's job easier; no longer would Puffer have viewed Sloan's position as merely a professional opinion. Instead, Sloan's position would have reflected the professional opinions of the city of Boston. At present, more urban renewal projects in Boston are being initiated by the private sector than in the public sector. This would be an ideal time to change BRA's approach to design review by developing specific written criteria. This would prevent disputes between BRA and architects in the future.

Notes

1. John Sloan (1980). Personal conversation, May 2.
2. *Ibid.*

3. Boston Redevelopment Authority (1974). *Memorandum* from John Sloan, Urban Designer, to Joe Berlandi, BRA Administration, October 24.

4. *Ibid.*

5. Sloan (1980).

6. Richard Puffer (1980). Personal conversation, April 25.

7. *Ibid.*

8. Sloan (1980).

9. *Ibid.*

10. *Ibid.*

11. Boston Redevelopment Authority (1975). *Memorandum* from John Sloan to George Weidenfeller, March 7.

12. Anthony J. Yudis (1975). "121A Looms Larger with Full Valuation." *Boston Sunday Globe*, March 16: A-49.

13. Robert Campbell (1977). "Charlestown Bank a Welcome Example of Good Ur-Bank Design." *Boston Sunday Globe*, April 10: Section H, p. 2.

14. Puffer (1980).

15. *Ibid.*

16. Sloan (1980).

10
Minneapolis: The Crossing

Since the early 1950s, urban design policies in Minneapolis have placed great emphasis on public and private cooperation. Today, private citizens actively participate in phases of the design review process and are encouraged to attend neighborhood meetings and public hearings on proposed projects. Furthermore, city urban designers include citizen input when they make recommendations on a proposed project. The city thus attempts to influence private development by creating a cooperative atmosphere in which the public and private sectors work together.

The active communication and cooperation of government planning officials and private citizens have resulted in a flexible, rather than rigid, urban design process, structured so as to ensure that design review would "provide the flexibility needed to allow diversity and creative design solutions."[1] City officials are cognizant of the many problems urban development encounters and feel that "professional expertise and adequate staff support" as well as "citizen and community input" are necessary components of effective design review.[2]

Including the Concept Plan Review Procedure as part of Minneapolis's Zoning Ordinance is further evidence of the city's commitment to sound urban design procedures. In fact, the City of Minneapolis Zoning Ordinance is unique in the sense that the city has devoted a section of its zoning ordinance to design review procedures. Urban design in Minneapolis is achieved through a project approach—the projects are individually reviewed by the urban designers of the Planning and Development Department. In fact, the Concept Plan Review Procedure can be regarded as a continuation of Minneapolis's past urban design policies: the partnership between the public and private sectors continues to be a crucial component of the process. The Concept Plan Review "serves as a vehicle for neighborhood and development expression that will lessen the probability of misunderstanding between the two parties."[3] It attempts to enhance cooperation and communication between the community and the developer by providing opportunities for these two groups to interact during the review process.

The first building development under the Concept Plan Review is The Crossing, a commercial/office/residential building located on a one-and-a-quarter acre site. Ted Glasrud Associates, owner and developer of The Crossing, also contracted to construct the building. James Stageberg, Partner-in-Charge and Roger W. Kipp, Architect, the Hodne/Stageberg Partners, were the architects of the project. Construction of The Crossing began late in 1979 and is projected to be completed by early 1981.

The Crossing will be a 17-story highrise located in the east half-block bounded by Second Avenue South, South Third Street, Marquette Avenue South, and Washington Avenue South (see Figs. 10-1 to 10-3). The west half of the block is occupied by the IBM office building.[4] The highrise will consist of 305 condominiums, a ground level retail area, a mixture of retail and office space on the skyway level, and 223 residential parking spaces in the basement level (see Figs. 10-4 and 10-5). The residential use of this building is partitioned into 220 one bedroom condominiums, 68 two bedroom condominiums, and 17 three bedroom condominiums (see Figs. 10-6 and 10-7).[5]

The overall appearance of the building will be similar to a capital letter L:

> The stories of residential units will define the "L" shape, and rest atop and to the edge of a 2-story block of retail space. The residential portion will overlook the landscaped rooftop of the retail portion; this plaza will also contain some recreational amenities such as shuffleboard courts and deck tennis. A 2-story atrium will cut through the retail and office space, beginning at the ground and ending in a skylight at the roof. Provisions have been made to accommodate skyway connections in all four directions (see Figs. 10-5 and 10-6).[6]

The only controversial issue that arose during the design review concerned the provision of parking space. Ted Glasrud Associates first submitted design plans for a mixed use building that included sufficient parking spaces but changed the original proposal shortly after it was approved by the City Planning Commission. The first

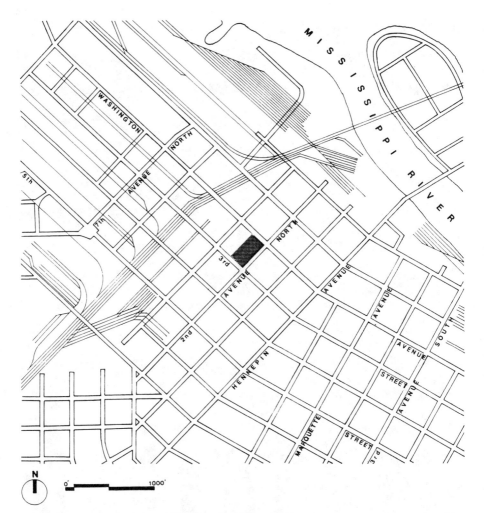

Figure 10-1: Location of site of The Crossing, Minneapolis

and second proposals were similar, except that the latter included additional residential use in the proposed building. Some additional parking space was provided in the second proposal but not enough to satisfy requirements of an amendment to Minneapolis's Zoning Code that was passed shortly after the first proposal was reviewed and accepted. The developer and architect of The Crossing worked with the Concept Plan Review members of the Office of Planning and Development and eventually came to a mutually acceptable agreement.

Figure 10-2: The Crossing, view of model at Second Avenue South and South Third Street
Source: The Hodne/Stageberg Partners Inc. and Ted Glasrud and Associates

Figure 10-3: The Crossing, view of model from rear elevation looking at the landscaped yard
Source: The Hodne/Stageberg Partners Inc. and Ted Glasrud and Associates

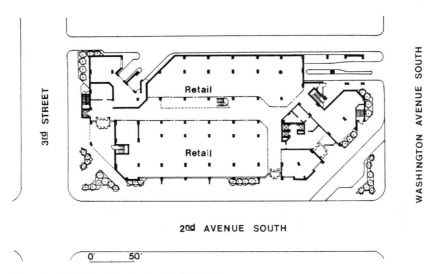

Figure 10-4: The Crossing, ground floor plan

Source: The Hodne/Stageberg Partners, Inc. and Ted Glasrud and Associates—Redrawn to the above scale

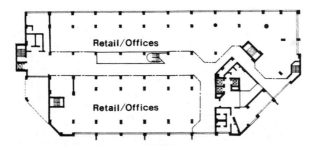

Figure 10-5: The Crossing, second floor plan, retail and office space at skyway level

Source: The Hodne/Stageberg Partners Inc. and Ted Glasrud and Associates—Redrawn to the above scale

The following individuals from the Minneapolis Department of Planning and Development were involved in the Concept Plan Review for The Crossing: Robert Eidem, Planner; Neil Anderson, Urban Designer; and William Nordrum, Urban Designer and Zoning Administrator. James Stageberg, Partner-in-Charge, and Roger W. Kipp, Architect of Hodne/Stageberg Partners, and a representative from Ted Glasrud Associates, owner and developer, were also members of the Concept Plan Review team.

Ted Glasrud Associates first submitted a development plan that consisted of two floors of retailing/office space and eleven floors of

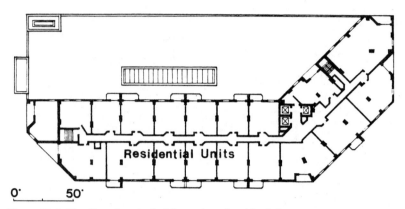

Figure 10-6: The Crossing, typical floor plan of residential space

Source: The Hodne/Stageberg Partners Inc. and Ted Glasrud and Associates—Redrawn to the above scale

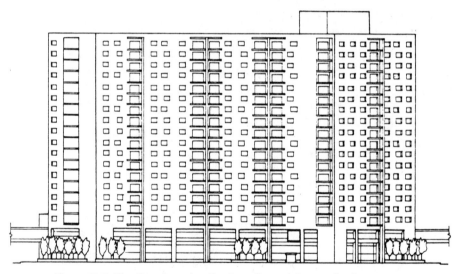

Figure 10-7: The Crossing, elevation from Second Avenue South

Source: The Hodne/Stageberg Partners Inc. and Ted Glasrud and Associates—Redrawn to the above scale

condominium apartments. The proposed project's site plans were acceptable to the staff of the Department of Planning and Development with one exception—the proposal did not conform to the Land Use Plan as adopted by the Planning Commission which designated the site as "General Commercial." The staff members of the Department of Planning and Development were reluctant to have the City Planning Commission change the zoning of the site to permit both residential and commercial use.[7] The Department of Planning and Development sent a memorandum to the City Planning Commission which stated:

> The Commission has before it a proposal to modify the Gateway Center Urban Renewal Plan and the city Land Use Plan to permit residential development on this site; the proposal would change the block's designation to "Commercial-Residential."[8]

The members of the Concept Review team were satisfied with The Crossing's proposed exterior appearance and features and underground parking provisions.[9] They were also satisfied with the information that Ted Glasrud Associates and the Hodne/ Stageberg Partners provided during the design review on (1) the population served; (2) need, compatibility, and appropriateness of the project; and (3) the environmental effects.

The following information relative to these three issues, required to be submitted during the Concept Plan Review, was appropriately supplied by Ted Glasrud Associates and his architects:

> 1. The residential portion of this building will attract persons and families of a wide range of incomes. The predominant market is expected to be comprised of middle income couples . . . the skyway system will also be attractive to retired households and single individuals.
> 2. The proposed development will increase home ownership opportunities in the city as well as reducing energy consumption, increasing the 24-hour activity level in the area, and increasing the supply of housing without the loss of any units in the process.
> 3. The predominant land use on the area is office/commercial. Major residential development has occurred to the east of the site. These developments provide subsidied and market rate rentals and condominium units.
> 4. The proposed development which combines commercial, office, and residential uses represents the best use of the property.
> 5. We anticipate no adverse environmental consequences of proceeding with the development as proposed.
> 6. The project will have a positive environmental impact resulting from: the creation of substantial new housing opportunities within walking or easy transit distance of substantial employment opportunities. This will reduce dependance upon automobile transportation and will relieve pressure for continued suburban sprawl.[10]

Oliver E. Byrum, Director of the Department of Planning and Development, arranged for the *Minneapolis Star and Tribune* to publish notice of a public meeting to be held on November 1, 1978.

The purpose of this public meeting was to consider the concept plan for the proposed building.[11] Only one person, a St. Paul architect, attended the meeting, and all his questions appeared to be answered to his satisfaction. The Concept Plan Review staff recommended the approval of Ted Glasrud's concept plan on November 9, but the staff's approval was contingent on the modification of the Land Use Plan.[12] The Concept Plan proposal was approved by the City Planning Commission on November 9, 1978.[13]

Before Ted Glasrud Associates began to make construction plans, it became more evident that the demand for residential space in downtown Minneapolis was growing. Indeed, since many of the buildings under construction in the downtown area were office buildings, Ted Glasrud Associates could show that the demand for residential space was not being met. Consequently, Ted Glasrud Associates approached the Department of Planning and Development and asked to change the initial proposal to a "17 story highrise of 305 condominium units and 2 stories of retail (approximately 68,000 square feet of floor area)"[14] (see Figs. 10-8 to 10-10). The exterior appearance and features of The Crossing were to remain the same as the first concept plan. However, there was another complicating factor. Since the developer submitted the first concept plan, the City Council had amended Chapter 540.1790 of the zoning code. As of April 21, 1979, the code required additional off-street parking for new developments in B4 districts (in which The Crossing's site was located). The developer proposed to provide 223 underground parking spaces for the residential units and retail spaces in the second proposal—29.5 fewer parking spaces than the 252.50 spaces required under the amended zoning ordinance.[15] The members of the Concept Plan Review team felt:

> The previous plan conformed to the parking requirements of the Zoning Ordinance. . . . Subsequently, an amendment has been adopted increasing the off-street parking requirement . . . , and as a result, the new proposal is 29½ spaces short of the new requirement. In view that the City changed the parking requirements after approval of the plan, and in view that the new plan provided a significantly larger number of spaces . . . , staff recommends that the strict provisions of the ordinance not be applied.[16]

The Department of Planning and Development felt that traffic generated from the project would have no adverse effect on

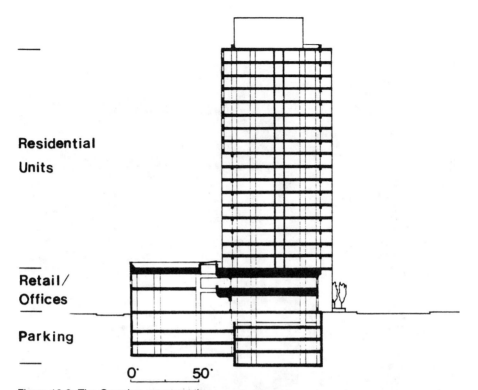

Residential

Units

Retail/
Offices

Parking

0'   50'

Figure 10-8: The Crossing, cross-section
Source: The Hodne/Stageberg Partners Inc. and Ted Glasrud and Associates—Redrawn to the above scale

Figure 10-9: The Crossing, view from model looking at landscaped yard (model)
Source: The Hodne/Stageberg Partners, Inc. and Ted Glasrud and Associates

Figure 10-10: The Crossing, overall view (model)

Source: The Hodne/Stageberg Partners Inc. and Ted Glasrud and Associates

adjacent properties and that the issues discussed relevant to population served; need, compatibility, and appropriateness of the project; and environmental effects for the first design scheme were applicable to the second scheme.[17] Ted Glasrud Associates' second proposal did not go through a complete Concept Plan Review because the main issues surrounding the project did not change; but a second neighborhood concept plan public meeting was held on May 3, 1979. Three property owners attended this meeting and expressed concern over the skyway system, landscaping on Washington Avenue, and the possible traffic congestion on Washington Avenue that might be generated because of the underground parking. Once again, the questions were answered to these persons' satisfaction.[18]

On May 10, 1979 the City Planning Cmmission held a public meeting on The Crossing, but no one was present to speak for or against the proposal. The Commissioners "moved to concur with staff [Department of Planning and Development] recommendation that the plan is in conformance with the Comprehensive Plan for the Central Business District, and to approve" the concept plan.[19] On May 30, 1979, Mayor Albert J. Hofstede approved the second proposal, and construction of The Crossing began late in 1979.[20]

Even though the construction of The Crossing is not completed to date, a number of design factors lead one to believe that the building will be successful. In particular, the skyway connection planned for The Crossing will be a significant aid to year-round pedestrian movement. It has been estimated that an average of 7,000 people pass through each skyway in Minneapolis each day, with 18,000 people using it in the winter months (see Fig. 10-11).[21] Furthermore, providing retail space in the first and second level of the building and residential in the remainder brings 24-hour activity to this section of the downtown area, and the landscaped courtyard provides a pleasing public amenity (see Figs. 10-9 and 10-10).

No major difficulties arose during the six-week Concept Plan Review for The Crossing. The urban designers of the Department of Planning and Development were more concerned over functional aspects of urban design than aesthetic concerns. Their interest in obtaining information on the population served by the project; the need, compatibility, and appropriateness of the project;and environmental impacts stemming from The Crossing illustrate this.

Furthermore, Minneapolis's Planning Department emphasized functional issues as outlined in the city's Comprehensive Plan and Minneapolis's Plan for the 1990s. Minneapolis's officials felt, for example, that

> newly constructed dwelling units . . . play a vital role in fostering after hours downtown life [and that] a balanced range of housing is the key variable in creating a twenty-four hour active, secure downtown.[22]

Thus, the Department of Planning and Development's urban

Figure 10-11: A section of Minneapolis's Skyway System

designers closely followed Minneapolis's long-range goals when considering issues for The Crossing.

Halpern says that architecture in Minneapolis "is not sculpture in the classical sense."[23] He feels that the Minneapolis officials have the following perspective of urban design:

> Buildings are not objects on a plaza to be admired. First and foremost, buildings are to be used by people—both those who work within a particular building and those who work around it. A building must therefore function accordingly by becoming an integral part of the urban environment. This accomplished, a building can then be "distinguished" and provide space which is "exciting" to see and be a part of but it must be space that, like the building, is usable.[24]

A factor which influences design review in Minneapolis that should not be underestimated is the long-term trust which exists between the public officials and the city. The trust and cooperation of the citizens of Minneapolis's predominantly Scandinavian population may have had a strong influence in cultivating a cooperative relationship between the public officials and the people. This cultural factor also may accent the people's concern for a better living environment and a high quality of life.

Citizens in Minneapolis can participate in city planning affairs by joining Planning District Citizen Advisory Committees.[25] These groups can devise methods for representing their neighborhoods and thus participate in city planning. However, despite the numerous avenues available for Minneapolis's citizens to express their opinions about planning issues, The Crossing case study found that few people chose to participate in the public hearing for the proposed project. The fact that only a few people went to the public hearings tends to illustrate the trust that the citizens place in their public officials to accept appropriate new development for downtown Minneapolis. Strong cooperative efforts between private and public agencies working together over the years to produce successful urban designs has also instilled trust. On the other hand, the poor public attendance at the public hearings may also be a reflection of citizen apathy.

Also contributing to successful design reviews in Minneapolis is the fact that the design review process is discussed very clearly in the city's zoning. Describing the design review process step by step saves the developer and architect valuable time and effort and consequently helps to create and maintain a friendly working relationship throughout the entire design review process.

Minneapolis's practice of updating planning studies on a periodic basis enables public officials to know what the city's needs and wants are at all times.[26] As the city makes progress toward achieving its goals and objectives and as economic, demographic, or other conditions change, updating regulations helps to maintain the relevance and utility of the regulations.

Notes

1. Minneapolis Department of Planning and Development (1979a). *Plan for the 1980's: Physical Environment*, p. 92.

2. *Ibid.*, p. 100.

3. *City of Minneapolis Zoning Ordinance* (1976). Concept Plan Review Procedure, Section 534.450, (2), (a), p. 3778.

4. Minneapolis Department of Planning and Development (1978a). *Memorandum* to the City Planning Commission, "Concept Plan Review for HRA Parcel 16b, Gateway Center," November, p. 1.

5. *Ibid.*, pp. 1, 4.

6. *Ibid.*, p. 1.

7. *Ibid.*

8. *Ibid.*

9. *Ibid.*

10. Minneapolis Department of Planning and Development (n.d.). *Memorandum* to the City Planning Commission, "Concept Plan Review for HRA Parcel 16b, Gateway Center," p. 4.

11. O. E. Byrum (1975). Letter to Carlton Gavick, *Minneapolis Star and Tribune,* October 12.

12. Minneapolis Department of Planning and Development (1978), p. 2.

13. Minneapolis Department of Planning and Development (n.d.), p. 1.

14. *Ibid.*

15. *Ibid.*, p. 2.

16. *Ibid.*

17. *Ibid.*, pp. 2–3.

18. *Ibid.*, p. 1.

19. Minneapolis Department of Planning and Development (1979*b*). Minutes of City Planning Commissioner's meeting, May 10.

20. *Minneapolis Star,* May 25, 1979.

21. Kenneth Halpern (1978). *Downtown USA: Urban Design in Nine American Cities* (New York: Whitney Library of Design), p. 225.

22. Minneapolis Department of Planning and Development (1978*b*). *Minneapolis Metro Center: Forecasts to 1990,* p. 24.

23. Halpern (1978), p. 223.

24. *Ibid.*

25. Minneapolis Department of Planning and Development (1979*a*), p. 47.

26. *Ibid.*, p. 44.

11

New York City: Olympic Tower

During the 1960s retail activity in New York City began to shift away from Fifth Avenue and was replaced by such institutional uses as banks, airlines, and corporate offices. As these institutional uses became more predominant, land values escalated until developers could only afford to build office buildings on the Avenue. Consequently, residential and retail facilities began to gravitate elsewhere; Fifth Avenue began to operate on a nine-to-five shift.[1]

Public and private opposition to the changing nature of Fifth Avenue led to the adoption of the FASD on March 26, 1971. When the OMPD urban designers and the CPC's legal staff wrote the district legislation, they tried to minimize the discretion that urban designers could exercise during the design review. This was accomplished by including all the design issues that the city was concerned about in the legislation. In contrast to previous special districts that were created in New York City, such as the Theatre District, the OMPD urban designers attempted to make the FASD nondiscretionary.

The principal goal of the FASD was to encourage residential and retail uses along Fifth Avenue. OMPD did not intend to prohibit construction of office buildings along Fifth Avenue; in fact, with the high value of land along the Avenue, it was felt that a retail store would only be profitable as part of a much larger structure. Furthermore, including residential units in the office buildings would increase the after-business-hours use of the Avenue.[2] The city intended to achieve the goal of the FASD largely by offering developers incentives in the form of floor area bonuses. A developer would be awarded two to 14 square feet for each square foot of public amenity included in the building. An additional 20% in FAR and an increase in lot coverage of 10% would be awarded if even more residential, hotel, and retail uses were included in the building.[3]

Olympic Tower was the first multi-use building constructed on Fifth Avenue in accordance with FASD regulations. Arthur Cohen, President of the Arlen Realty and Development Corporation, owned the building site jointly with Victory Carriers, Inc., an Onassis family trust. Whitson Overcash, Partner-in-Charge, and Paul Baron, Project Manager, of Skidmore, Owings, & Merrill designed the building; Tishman Realty and Construction Co., Inc., was responsible for the construction. Max Siegel of Max Siegel Associates represented the owners on zoning and coding issues relating to the design plan of Olympic Tower.[4]

Olympic Tower, located on the northeast corner of Fifth Avenue and East 51st Street, is situated between two landmarks—St. Patrick's Cathedral and Cartier (see Figs. 11-1 and 11-2). The 52-story building contains two floors of retail space, office space on 17 levels, residential units on the remaining 30 floors, a shopping arcade, and a plaza with a waterfall on the ground floor[5] (see Figs. 11-3 to 11-5). Skidmore, Owings, & Merrill (hereafter referred to as SOM) employed a new construction technique for this building— the retail and office sections of the building were constructed with steel, while the residential units consisted of concrete. This is one of the first buildings constructed with multiple materials.[6]

Commercial space in Olympic Tower totals 46.6% of the floor area, and the 30 floors of residential use represents 53% of the total area.[7] Olympic Tower was designed to take full advantage of the FASD bonuses. For instance, the design of Olympic Tower included an air-conditioned and covered pedestrian space that qualified for 11.0 square feet of floor area bonuses as compared to 10.0 square feet of bonuses for an open pedestrian space. In addition, the building provided extra retail and residential floor area to take advantage of the maximum FAR allowed by the special district zoning.

A covered pedestrian space, however, does have certain disadvantages associated with it: it is less attractive and offers fewer public amenities. An open plaza pedestrian through-way provides more public amenities because its openness invites people to come inside the building. This design also enables

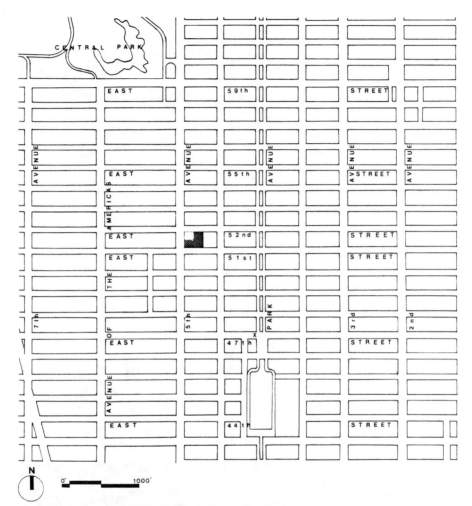

Figure 11-1: Location of site of Olympic Tower, New York

people passing the building to know what is going on inside. Lastly, since the builder is given fewer bonuses for providing an open pedestrian through-way, the building will be shorter and therefore have less negative visual impact.

By providing retail and residential space in excess of the minimum requirement stated in the FASD as well as the pedestrian through-block connection, Olympic Tower was built with a FAR of 21.6 or 40,417.71 square feet. Under the provisions of the FASD, the developers were required to provide between a minimum FAR 3.6 and a maximum FAR 12 in residential use, FAR 1.9 of retail

Figure 11-2: Olympic
Tower, situated between St.
Patrick's Cathedral and
Cartier

Source: Office of The Midtown Planning and Development

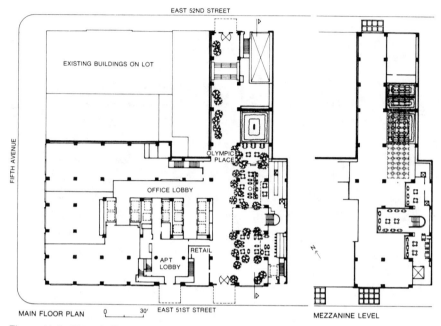

Figure 11-3: Olympic Tower, main floor plan

Reprinted from the December 1975 issue of *Progressive Architecture*, copyright 1975, Reinhold Publishing.

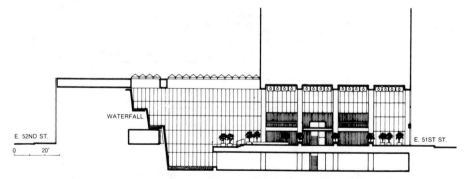

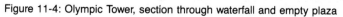

Figure 11-4: Olympic Tower, section through waterfall and empty plaza

Reprinted from the December 1975 issue of *Progressive Architecture*, copyright 1975, Reinhold Publishing.

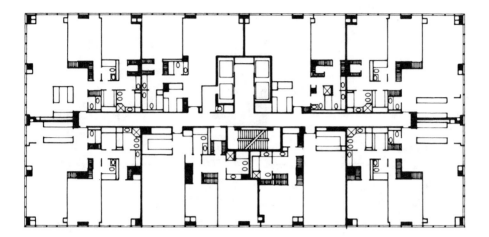

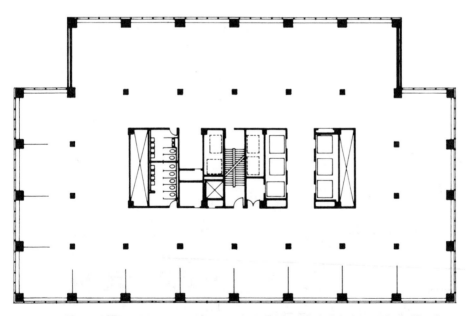

Figure 11-5: Olympic Tower: above, typical residential plan; below, typical office floor plan

Reprinted from the December 1975 issue of *Progressive Architecture*, copyright 1975, Reinhold Publishing.

area, and a minimum of 8,600 square feet for a pedestrian through-block connection.[8]

The major design issues concerning Olympic Tower were the following:

1. Encouraging retail activity on the ground floor level;
2. Providing as much window-shopping space as possible;
3. Building Olympic Tower up to the lot line in order to preserve the "wall" of Fifth Avenue;
4. Designing a public space that is open to the side streets; and
5. Including retailing in the basement and/or on the second floor of the building and connecting the retail-use floors with an escalator.

The main controversy that occurred during the design review process involved the developer's resistance to providing sufficient amounts of retail space. However, after extended meetings with members of the OMPD, the developer decided to provide the retail space, at least partly for the following reason: because the front-end costs were rising rapidly, the developer foresaw the economic advantages of maximizing the amount of residential floor area, and Arthur Cohen thought he might be able to interest a department store in taking all of the retail space.[9]

The members of the design review team in the Olympic Tower case were Jacquelin Robertson, Urban Designer and Director of the Office of Midtown Planning and Development; Stephen Quick, Senior Urban Designer, OMPD; Al Schimmel, Real Estate Consultant, City Planning Department; and several members of the Planning Commission's legal staff. Whitson Overcash, Partner-in-Charge, and Paul Baron, Project Manager, Skidmore, Owings, & Merrill; Max Siegel, Max Siegel Associates; and Arthur Cohen, Chairman, and Arthur Levine, President, Arlen Realty and Development Corporation, represented the developers.

OMPD's Robertson and Quick were directly involved in the design review process for Olympic Tower. The main goal of the OMPD urban designers was to maintain the quality of Fifth Avenue's retailing character; hence, the design review focused chiefly on how to achieve this goal.

Final design proposals for Olympic Tower submitted by Arlen Realty indicated that they were interested in taking full advantage of the FASD bonuses. Although the FASD was not officially incorporated in New York City's Zoning Ordinance until March 26,

1971, city officials were anxious for the Olympic Tower project to include aspects of the special district. During the time the design plans were being negotiated for Olympic Tower, "representatives of the Olympic Tower . . . were directly involved in the development of the special district regulations."[10]

Siegel suggested during a design review session that the building should be handled by special permit because he was uncertain if the special district legislation would be passed in time. At first Siegel desired a special permit only for the covered pedestrian space; he later suggested handling height and setback and residential FAR by special permit as well because of the delays he foresaw.[11] At a December 22, 1970 design review meeting, Robertson and Quick suggested not to "tie the special permit requirements to any particular bonus, but rather provide a list giving discrimination to the CPC on each particular amenity and site."[12] This position was ultimately dropped in favor of the special district legislation.

The design proposal submitted by SOM included many features of the proposed FASD, but there were a number of issues which had to be worked out. In particular, the two sets of drawings submitted to the Building Department and the CPC did not provide a detailed design of the building's arcade. Furthermore, the plans contained only a note stating that a certain amount of retailing would be provided. Quick noted in a memorandum that Siegel "did not like the 100,000 square foot retail request in the draft of 12-4-70. . . . that such a figure jeopardizes Cohen's bargaining position for any department store."[13]

On December 16, 1970, Siegel presented another version of the design plans to the OMPD. OMPD reviewed the plans and found "the plans met with general favorable approval, although [there were] problems with the amount of retail space provided and the Olympic Airways ground floor space."[14]

Siegel continued to stress that

> the 1:1 provision [1:1 refers to one square foot of retail space for each square foot of lot area] in the special permit as proposed was too much and suggested a 3:1 ratio [3:1 refers to one square foot of retail space for every three feet of lot area] or else 7 percent of total bulk of the commercial floor area be devoted to retail use.[15]

This caused concern at OMPD, and again the urban designers were uncertain if Cohen would remain committed to providing a department store in the Olympic Tower. Seven percent of the total commercial floor area in retail uses would amount to slightly less than 50,000 square feet.[16] This figure is substantially less than the 76,793.64 square feet that the FASD mandates.[17]

On December 18, 1970, Schimmel met with Arthur Cohen to find out the economic rationale behind Cohen's request to devote "a minimum of 7 percent of total commercial floor area for specified retail uses as a condition for obtaining bonus floor area which would be utilized for residential purposes."[18] Cohen stressed that he would suffer economic losses, which could not be recouped by the bonus residential area, for every square foot of space that he is required to reserve for a department store. Cohen presented figures to back up his position; however, when Schimmel set up his own calculations to test the validity of Cohen's statement, he found he could not duplicate Cohen's findings. In fact, Schimmel felt "it is difficult to understand why the Cohen-Onassis group is even considering . . . substituting ground floor space to be reserved for a development store for bonus space to be devoted to luxury apartment units."[19]

At this point, Cohen stated his front-end costs were increasing rapidly and that "he would proceed along conventional lines" if necessary to expedite the process. Cohen also added that he "hoped to get the prospective store tenants to take more than 50,000 minimum square feet, but would not or could not state that the current negotiations to bring a department store to the site would be successful."[20]

Schimmel came to two conclusions after his meeting with Arthur Cohen. First, economic loss would be mitigated if retail use was included in the basement space. But Schimmel felt that

> we need not fear that a developer will attempt to fulfill his requirements by putting all or most of the required retail space in the basement. Any respectable department store will insist on ground floor space plus upper floor space in preference to basement space. We could also provide that in order to qualify for the zoning bonus, a specified percentage of the required retail space must be ground.[21]

Second, Schimmel noted that a bonus of 3.5 FAR in additional office space instead of residential space would cover the losses over which Cohen was concerned. At this point, Schimmel wondered: "Is it possible that this is the direction in which we will ultimately be requested to move?"[22]

On December 23, 1970, Schimmel reported his findings of the

Cohen meeting at an OMPD meeting. The information caused uneasiness within the group. Quick reported that Schimmel expected "that Cohen will come in at the last minute with a request for a 20 percent increase in office space."[23]

On January 14, 1971, Quick met with Siegel and William Bardel, OMPD's deputy director. Siegel provided a list of seven points he thought should be listed in the district legislation included in this list was "the amount of retail space be expressed in a percentage of the allowable bulk."[24] Siegel also stated requirements which would be best suited to the Olympic Tower site and the rest of the district—one of which included "7 percent of allowable bulk as the minimum retail requirement."[25] Quick noted that

> Max [Siegel] is seeking for Cohen a 21.6 FAR building with 7 FAR [plus] residential and a maximum retail commitment of 47,000 square feet. When asked if he is conveying Mr. Cohen's position, Max became quite evasive saying he had, of course, been hired by Cohen to protect his interests, but he feels he is just as much a consultant for all of the Fifth Avenue interests.[26]

Cohen did not attempt to use external power to reduce the amount of retail space that he was required to provide in the Olympic Tower. For instance, Mayor Lindsay strongly supported the district legislation; therefore, it was highly unlikely that the mayor would be sympathetic to Cohen's request to decrease the retail space requirement. Cohen was also no doubt aware that previous attempts by developers to bypass the Planning Department were unsuccessful. Nor did the urban designers of OMPD need to use external force—the design issues they were concerned about were in the FASD legislation. The elimination of discretionary power in the FASD legislation prohibited the urban designers from delving into the design details of the building but did enable them to remain steadfast on the retail space requirements since these were outlined in the FASD.

The planning review lasted approximately one year, with the majority of the time spent on the design review. Construction of Olympic Tower began in August, 1971. The building finally had a FAR of 21.6 by taking advantage of all of the bonuses provided in the FASD.[27] Olympic Tower was built as-of-right; therefore, a building permit rather than a special permit or variance was granted by the Department of Building after a zoning review by the city. This occurred because the Special District regulations permitted a FAR up to 21.6 through stipulations and the provision of amenities. Traditional zoning does not permit the CPC to grant variances—the Board of Standards and Appeals has this authority. However, the CPC has discretionary power over the regulations it has developed. The maximum FAR in the FASD was set at 21.6, and therefore the Commission had the power to approve the design of Olympic Tower as long as the design did not exceed FAR 21.6.[28]

There are two main problems with Olympic Tower. First, an escalator connecting the ground floor to the second floor was never built, even though it was included in the original design of the building. Instead, the developer and the architect changed the design and replaced the escalator with a waterfall. The waterfall, however, did not qualify for the same floor area bonus of 3.0 square feet that was awarded for the escalator; but the developer received the 3.0 square foot bonus anyway and ended negotiations with a total bonus of 14.0 square feet when theoretically the bonuses should have only totalled 11.0 square feet. The CPC should have reduced the floor area bonus, but instead they approved the design. Furthermore, Olympic Tower has only 92,000 square feet of covered pedestrian space instead of the 120,000 square feet prescribed in the FASD regulations.

The second problem with Olympic Tower has to do with insufficient retailing space being provided in the building. Retailing should have been included in the basement level, ground floor, and second floor of Olympic Tower, but active retailing was only provided in the latter two levels. The basement level contains mostly inactive retailing. A restaurant is located in the basement, but it serves primarily the office workers in Olympic Tower, as well as acting as a service facility for the residents of the condominiums. The remainder of the basement houses a wine cellar, rental offices, and various storage areas for the shops on the ground level. In addition, the arcade located in the covered pedestrian space was counted towards the required retailing space, but the arcade remains predominantly empty (see Figs. 11-6 to 11-7). Additionally, the retailing opening into 51st Street has no entrance from the plaza and thus prohibits people from gaining access to the retail shops from the plaza (see Figs. 11-8 and 11-9). Lastly, while the waterfall at the plaza is very nice and adequate seating space is available, there are no associated uses for people using the plaza

Figure 11-6: Olympic Tower, empty plaza which was supposed to contain cafe and several small specialty shops

Figure 11-7: Olympic Tower: empty plaza, dead atmosphere

Figure 11-8: Olympic Tower: Plaza connecting 51st and 52nd Streets, looking at 51st Street entrance

Figure 11-9: Olympic Tower, retailing facing 51st Street with no entry from plaza

since the retail space and café were never provided (see Figs. 11-10 and 11-11).

It was the responsibility of the Building Department, rather than OMPD's urban designers or the CPC, to ensure that all elements shown on the design drawings were included in the final building. Lauren Otis, Deputy Director of OMPD who assumed Robertson's and Quick's responsibility for Olympic Tower after they left the department, feels that the city made an error with Olympic Tower.[29] Yet, it is difficult for building inspectors to ensure that the building space is used properly. Inspectors compare the design plan with the final product, the constructed building, to see if they match; but the inspector cannot determine at that point if the space will be used as originally specified. This cannot be ascertained until the building is fully completed and occupied.

Quick also feels that the problems with the final product—lack of a café and retail space adjacent to the covered pedestrian space—were basically the responsibility of the Building Department. However, he attributes some of the failures of the building to the poor cooperative working relationship and lack of postconstruction zoning review among the Building Department, the OMPD, and the Department of City Planning.[30]

Overall, critics view Olympic Tower negatively. Weaver and Babcock use Olympic Tower as an example of the way "a developer may comply with the letter of the law, earn bonuses and produce a design failure."[31] They also quote Ada Louise Huxtable, urban design critic of the *New York Times*, who has *no* illusions about developers: "New York builders are notoriously adept at formulating a package that satisfied the letter of the law and does the least to fulfill what city planners had in mind."[32]

Some feel that its "basic black box" look is not appropriate for a mixed use building.

> Its sleek, impassive, opaque skins and taut rectangular form now are associated too closely with a corporate office building. Not only is one not aware of the varying kinds of activities going on in the building from the exterior package, but there is scarcely a clue to their differentiation—where offices stop and residential begins (except for mechanical space). Perhaps that's the point. Its consummate elegance and restraint, perfect for the powerful corporate image, corresponds easily to the self-image and tastes of the very rich who will live there. . . . The small sedate apartment lobby is separate from the sedate office lobby.[33]

Figure 11-10: Olympic Tower: Plaza connecting 51st and 52nd Streets, looking at 52nd Street entrance

Figure 11-11: Olympic Tower: waterfall at plaza; no associated uses provided

The Olympic Tower is also of a different scale and appearance from the current character of Fifth Avenue. Saint Patrick's Cathedral is dwarfed by the height of the Olympic Tower, and the brick or stone covering of the surrounding buildings is quite different from Olympic Tower's black glass (see Fig. 11-12). In fact,

> the indifference in which the Olympic Tower related to the low-scale turn-of-the-century structures [on the Avenue] shows more of a concern for meeting the new zoning requirements [FASD] and certain programmatic needs, than an attempt to acknowledge the architectural context through massing, configuration, and materials.[34]

In addition to architectural concerns, the height of the Olympic Tower may block a portion of the sunlight that originally fell on the Avenue. Okamoto and Williams contend that Fifth Avenue is relatively low amid the skyscrapers, and this allows more sunlight to fall on window shoppers.[35]

The main controversy during the design review concerned the amount of retail space provided in Olympic Tower. Since decreasing retail use on Fifth Avenue was one of the major reasons for creating the FASD, it is understandable that Robertson and Quick were unwilling to accept Cohen's suggestion to decrease retail space in Olympic Tower by almost 30,000 square feet. Quick and Robertson had a difficult time getting Cohen to change his mind on the retail use issue for two reasons. First, urban designers of OMPD serve in an advisory function; hence, until the FASD legislation was adopted, they did not have the authority to insist that Cohen provide more retail space than he had shown in his original design proposal. The second reason arises from the fact that the FASD regulations were still in the planning stage during the beginning of the design review; this may have encouraged Cohen to resist providing the additional retail space—especially since Siegel was actively involved in designing the regulations. Cohen may have been dragging his feet in hope that the regulations concerning retail space requirements would be revised.

At face value, the OMPD and the City Planning Commission were protecting the interests of the general public, but economic and political pressures were probably stronger forces. Former Mayor Lindsay, OMPD, and public and private organizations strongly supported the FASD. By changing the economic variables a builder considers when planning to build a new structure, it was

Figure 11-12: One can easily observe the incompatibility of Olympic Tower in juxtaposition with St. Patrick's Cathedral

Figure 11-13: Olympic Tower: the only positive aspect, preservation of retailing, at the ground level, Fifth Avenue

hoped that multiple-use buildings would be attracted to Fifth Avenue. The Fifth Avenue Association also strongly supported the FASD. They felt that "high-fashion and luxury shops on the Avenue . . . were the prime attractions that drew millions of dollars of tourist business to New York each year."[36] Likewise, the success of the Special Theatre District created in the Times Square area made Association members want a similar device to encourage retailing on Fifth Avenue. The officials of the City Planning Commission were also strongly in favor of the FASD because it was felt that mixed-use buildings "would stimulate economics in the midtown area."[37]

As stated previously, Olympic Tower appears to appeal to the élite rather than to the general public. This may have occurred in part because the public officials of New York were almost obsessed with solving the economic problems of Fifth Avenue and consequently seemed to lose sight of providing public amenities that would appeal to the public at large. Cook's criticism of what he calls "elective controls" (e.g., incentive bonuses) could apply here: "By conceding the right to a fixed density in advance at a given site, a city has already lost a major urban-design battle and is left with only details to negotiate."[38] Quick, however, feels that the FASD legislation actually provides more public amenities than other special districts in New York and definitely more than the basic ordinance.[39] On the other hand, Cohen and SOM likely sensed that they were holding the "trump card." Newspaper coverage of the proposed Olympic Tower more or less reflected public officials' views that Olympic Tower, if successful, could be the "savior" of the Avenue. Thus, Cohen may have been inadvertently given a little more bargaining power during the design review than was intended.

Part of the problem may also stem from the lack of discretionary power given to the urban designers of OMPD. They were solely advisory in nature and could not legally disapprove of any component of the design. Additionally, the FASD regulations were created to be rather flexible so as to respond to market and social conditions of the Avenue. Thus, the developer and architect were given a fair amount of leeway in designing the building, but the design review staff was limited in exerting any pressure except on issues discussed in the district legislation.

On the surface FASD may appear a simple mechanism, but in reality it is a complex with many interrelationships that may serve to strengthen a number of the desired design and use elements. For example, a developer can qualify for up to 21.6 FAR by providing Elective Lot Improvements and additional retail and residential space in the building. Only 3.6 FAR is required for residential use, but this is not enough floor area to be economically feasible. The developer will be thus inclined to provide additional residential space—approximately 10 FAR to 12 FAR—to make the project viable. Olympic Tower, for example, has 12.0 FAR in residential use, even though the FASD only requires 3.6 FAR. In this case, then, incentive zoning achieved returns far in excess of the written legislation.

The FASD is also a preservation district. The legislation makes it very difficult for a developer to build up to 18 FAR, since it places many mandatory requirements on the development and is quite specific and restrictive on the kinds of public design amenities the building must provide. This means that the developer is not economically encouraged to tear down existing structures and will carefully think about building a speculative office building. But if the developer desires to build a structure that includes public amenities that the FASD encourages, the legislation acts as a true incentive and compensates the developer in the form of more floor space for these public gestures.

The fact that Otis replaced Robertson and Quick after the design review did not really have any effect on the outcome of Olympic Tower because the building was very close to completion when the change in staff took place. So far, the only positive aspect of Olympic Tower is preservation of retail space at street level, Fifth Avenue (see Fig. 11-13).

However, the Olymic Tower case is still continuing. Robertson, now in private architectural practice, is redesigning the arcade, trying to rectify all the previous deficiencies.[40] This could be a quite helpful step in bringing the project to a successful conclusion since Robertson was one of the major initiators of FASD.

Notes

1. Suzanne Stephens (1975). "Microcosms of Urbanity." *Progressive Architecture*, 56: 37–38.

2. Robert E. Davis and Jon Weston, eds. (1975). *The Special Zoning Concept*

in New York City (New York: New School for Social Research, Center for New York City Affairs), pp. 27–28.

3. *City of New York Zoning Ordinance* (1975). Special Fifth Avenue District, Chapter 7, Section 87-065, p. 417 and Sections 87–08 and 87–09, p. 418.

4. "Mixed-Use Buildings: Olympic Tower" (1975). *Progressive Architecture,* 56: 47.

5. *Ibid.,* 45.

6. Stanley Thea (n.d.) *Fact Sheet* (Arlen Realty and Development Corporation), pp. 3–4.

7. Davis and Weston (1975), p. 23.

8. *Ibid.,* p. 24.

9. Stephen Quick (1980). Personal conversation, May 13.

10. Davis and Weston (1975), p. 28.

11. New York Office of Midtown Planning and Development (1970*a*). *Memorandum* from Stephen Quick to staff, "Olympic Tower Building," December 1, p. 1. and Stephen Quick (1980). Personal conversation.

12. New York Office of Midtown Planning and Development (1970*b*). *Memorandum* from Stephen Quick to staff, "Best & Co. and 20% Residential," December 23, p. 2.

13. New York Office of Midtown Planning and Development (1970*c*). *Memorandum* from Stephen Quick to staff, "20% Residential Special Permit," December 7, 1970, p. 1.

14. New York Office of Midtown Planning and Development (1970*b*), p. 2.

15. New York Office of Planning and Development (1970*d*). *Memorandum* from Stephen Quick to staff, "Fifth Avenue and Best & Co. Site," December 16, p. 1.

16. New York Office of Midtown Planning and Development (1970*e*). *Memorandum* from Alfred Schimmel to Jaquelin Robertson, "The Best Site," December 21, p. 1.

17. Davis and Weston (1975), p. 24.

18. New York OMPD Office of Midtown Planning and Development (1970*e*), p. 1.

19. *Ibid.,* p. 4.

20. *Ibid.*

21. *Ibid.*

22. *Ibid.,* p. 5.

23. New York Office of Midtown Planning and Development (1970*b*), p. 1.

24. New York Office of Midtown Planning and Development (1970*f*).

Memorandum from Stephen Quick to staff, "Fifth Avenue and Best & Co. Site," January 14, p. 1.

25. *Ibid.*

26. *Ibid.*

27. Davis and Weston (1975), p. 24.

28. *Ibid.*, p. 85.

29. Lauren Otis (1980). Personal conversation, April 24.

30. Quick (1980). Personal conversation, May 13.

31. Clifford L. Weaver and Richard F. Babcock (1979). *City Zoning* (Chicago: American Planning Association), p. 299.

32. *Ibid.*, p. 301.

33. "Mixed-Use Buildings" (1975), 45.

34. *Ibid.*

35. Rai Y. Okamoto and Frank E. Williams (1968). *Urban Design Manhattan* (New York: The Viking Press), p. 58.

36. *New York Times* (1971). February 10.

37. *New York Post* (1971). August 24.

38. Robert S. Cook, Jr. (1979). *Zoning for Downtown Urban Design* (Lexington, Mass.: Lexington Books), p. 155.

39. Quick (1980). Personal conversation, May 13.

40. Jacquelin Robertson (1980). Personal conversation, June 9.

12

San Francisco: One Market Plaza

In 1971 urban design controls for San Francisco were incorporated into the city's overall master plan. Allan Jacobs, Director of the City Planning Department from 1967 to 1974, organized the urban design team which produced the urban design plan. Jacobs was interested in devising urban design guidelines that were practical and workable. Policies included in the zoning laws were automatically enforceable, while more ambiguous policies were subjected to discretionary design reviews conducted by the Department of City Planning.[1] The resultant urban design plan is divided into four major sections:

> the city pattern, which deals with issues of image and character, organization and sense of purpose and orientation for travel; the conservation section which encompasses the concerns for protection of natural areas, heritage resources and street spaces; a section dealing with major new development which establishes policies regarding visual harmony with the existing setting, height and bulk and special provisions for large development sites; and the neighborhood environment section which sets urban design requirements as related to health and safety, opportunities for recreation, visual amenity and neighborhood identification and association.[2]

San Francisco's urban design staff was particularly concerned with new buildings on Market Street and Union Square and authorized that all proposed buildings for these locations would be subject to design reviews.[3]

Given San Francisco's unique topography of hills, ocean, and splendid views, a portion of the 1971 urban design controls was aimed specifically at protecting views of the waterfront. In particular, height and bulk regulations as well as protection of view corridors were deemed crucial elements of quality design by the urban designers. Although height controls have been an integral part of San Francisco's zoning laws in the past, the city planners now stressed that building heights should taper down to the shoreline of the bay and ocean so as to protect views of the bay from the high points in the city. Another technique used to reduce the general obtrusiveness of new buildings is to regulate the width and diagonal dimensions of the buildings so that they would be thin and would not impede views of the city.[4] Both height and bulk controls are used successfully to protect view corridors—views down particular streets.

The Southern Pacific Land Company, a consolidated subsidiary of Southern Pacific Company, was responsible for directing the development of One Market Plaza. The Southern Pacific Company was directly involved in the project because it was not governed, as was the Southern Pacific Transportation Company, by strict Interstate Commerce Commission regulations which would preclude a number of the activities necessary in the construction of the building. Many intracompany transactions took place prior to the actual conceptualization of One Market Plaza.

First, the Southern Pacific Land Company, the sponsor of the project, purchased land from its parent Southern Pacific Company. An existing 11-story building located on the site has served as Southern Pacific's headquarters since 1917. The Southern Pacific Transportation Company owned the headquarters but leased the ground floor of the building to the Southern Pacific Land Company. Finally, the Southern Pacific Land Company, with full ownership of the land in hand, leased the land to One Market Plaza, Inc., the partnership set up for the development. The Equitable Life Insurance Society of the United States joined the Southern Pacific Land Company in forming the partnership of One Market Plaza, Inc. Both Equitable and Southern Pacific Land Company had an equal vote in decision making for One Market Plaza, but Equitable chose to remain minimally involved in the actual design of the project.[5]

Southern Pacific Company owned an entire block (2.7 acres) along Market Street, bounded by Market, Steuart, Mission, and Spear Streets (see Figs. 12-1 to 12-4). One Market Plaza consists of two towers, 28 and 43 stories respectively, located adjacent to Southern Pacific Transportation Company's existing 11-story build-

Figure 12-1: Location of site of One Market Plaza, San Francisco

ing (see Figs. 12-4). The old and new structures have a common six-story base "that covers most of the site and accommodates a large amount of floor space in several office levels."[6] The six-story base with a main entrance on Market Street opens into a galleria and pedestrian mall protected by a glass canopy. Southern Pacific Company occupies some of the new office floor space in One Market Plaza, but the majority is rental space.[7]

One Market Plaza incorporated all of the major objectives of the new urban design controls. O. G. Linde, President of Southern Pacific Land Company, and W. A. Finsterbusch, Southern Pacific

Figure 12-2: One Market Plaza from Market Street, main entrance

Figure 12-3: One Market Plaza from Steuart Street, illustrating connection of old and new structures

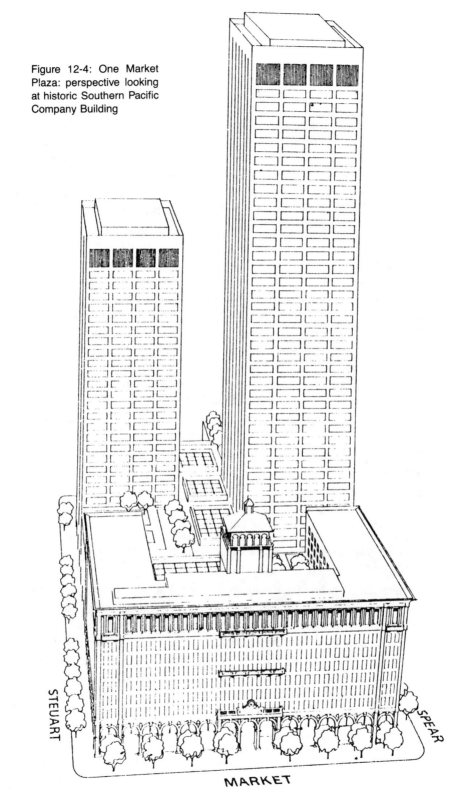

Figure 12-4: One Market Plaza: perspective looking at historic Southern Pacific Company Building

STEUART

SPEAR

MARKET

Source: One Market Plaza, a joint Venture of The Equitable Life Assurance Society of the United States and Southern Pacific Land Company.

project developer for One Market Plaza, were directly involved in all aspects of the planning stage. Welton Becket and Associates designed the building with the assistance of two San Francisco-based consulting structural engineering firms—Chin and Hensolt and H. J. Degenkolb & Associates. Galbreath-Ruffin Corporation and Clifton C. Brinkley Consultants were also involved in the project development. The contractor for the building was Dinwiddie-Turner, a joint venture between Dinwiddie Construction Company, San Francisco, and Turner Construction Company, New York City.[8]

The Southern Pacific Land Company realized that the Department of City Planning would exercise its discretionary design review powers over any development proposed after the City Planning Commission adopted Resolution No. 6111 in June 1967. This resolution "calls for discretionary review by the Commission of all new and enlarged buildings along Market Street."[9] Consequently, Southern Pacific chose to use a careful step-by-step approach to develop One Market Plaza. V. A. Wolfe, Manager, Real Estate Development, Southern Pacific Company, contacted San Francisco's Department of City Planning as early as February 14, 1967. An in-house City Planning Department memorandum indicated that

> Mr. Wolfe was in to talk about the SP [Southern Pacific] block on the Mission St. side. SP may be ready before long to build a rental office building on the eastern half. . . . I went over possible bonuses, development rights transfers, and possibility of the whole block being considered as one lot. There seems to be a lot of flexibility here.[10]

The Southern Pacific Company also asked the Department of City Planning to outline its urban design criteria for the site before they began to prepare preliminary design plans. Jacobs indicated that "Southern Pacific contacted the Department of City Planning last fall [1970], before the start of serious planning for the project."[11] Linde recalled that "We didn't even have any rough sketches of the proposed building before I went to see Allen [sic] Jacobs [then City Planner] to get his thoughts on guidelines for the development."[12]

The most significant design terms for One Market Plaza involved respecting the view corridors. Market Street divides two grid systems—views from both Pine and California Streets—which

Figure 12-5: One Market Plaza view corridors along California and Pine Streets
Source: One Market Plaza, a Joint Venture of The Equitable Life Assurance Society of the United States and Southern Pacific Land Company.

cross the Southern Pacific site. Jacobs felt it absolutely necessary to protect these views: "View corridors down California and Pine Streets to the Bay and the East Bay hills should be maintained, with particular attention to the outstanding view down California Street"[13] (see Fig. 12-5).

Linde appeared to agree with Jacob's assessment of the view corridors when he stated "We will not consider any plan which would have the effect of further blocking the view of the bay along the California and Pine Streets corridors."[14] Linde's feelings were carried over into the design review, and no lasting problems with blocking the view corridors occurred.

The Southern Pacific Company did express a desire to demolish the existing Southern Pacific headquarters, but agreed early in the design review to retain the building (see Figs. 12-6 and 12-7).[15] Aside from this one problem, the development of One Market Plaza was right in line with the Urban Design Guidelines formulated by the City Planning Department. Construction of One Market Plaza began in June, 1973 and was scheduled for completion in the spring of 1976.[16]

Figure 12-6: One Market Plaza, view from Spear Street illustrating connection to historic Southern Pacific Company Building

Figure 12-7: One Market Plaza blends historic and new structures with minimum impact on historic building

The members of the design review team for One Market Plaza were the following: Allan B. Jacobs, Director of the Department of City Planning; Dewayne Guyer and Richard Hedman, Urban Designers, Department of City Planning; Peter Svirsky, Legal Advisor, Department of City Planning; Richard Passmore, Zoning Administrator, Department of City Planning; W. A. Finsterbusch, Project Developer, Southern Pacific Company; O. G. Linde, President of Southern Pacific Company; Lawrence E. Hoyt, Vice President of Southern Pacific Company; and Nick Primiani, Partner-in-Charge, and Conley S. Weaver, Chief Architect, of Welton Becket and Associates, Architects.

Jacobs met with Hoyt on November 19, 1970, to discuss the Southern Pacific Headquarters site. At this point, Hoyt just wanted to discuss "preliminary site considerations (some of them dealing with design criteria)," although Hoyt did mention the possibility of "taking down the Market Street Building [the Southern Pacific Headquarters] eventually." Potential uses of the building—hotel, residential, offices, and retail—were also discussed during this meeting. Jacobs indicated that the Department of City Planning would be concerned with the following design issues: view corridor, height, bulk, and street facades.[17]

On December 10, 1970, Guyer sent an interoffice memorandum to Hedman and Svirsky which outlined preliminary design terms for the Southern Pacific Market Street site.[18] Many of Guyer's design terms were incorporated in a letter that Jacobs sent to Hoyt on December 11, 1970. The following excerpts from this letter illustrate the Department of City Planning's desire to work cooperatively with Southern Pacific:

> I am pleased to have this opportunity, at your request, to outline some of the principal considerations for development in the Southern Pacific Block bounded by Market, Spear, Mission and Steuart Streets.
> The urban design terms of reference attached to this letter are intended to help shape development according to the broader public aspects involved in relating buildings to one another and this site and the interests of Southern Pacific.
> The terms of reference are, of course, general and preliminary at this stage, and subject to further development in view of Southern Pacific's program as we understand it and the design solutions of your architects. We hope to have further discussions with you as such refinements occur.[19]

The attachment that Jacobs refers to in the letter was a four-page list of recommendations of urban design terms for the Southern Pacific site. Jacobs stressed that

> the entire block be considered as a unit . . . because such unified consideration would allow the greatest possible latitude for imaginative design solutions, . . . [and] would give a great deal of flexibility under the zoning requirements of the Downtown Office district, including use of building features for which floor area bonuses may be given.[20]

Jacobs did caution Southern Pacific that

> it is doubtful the maximum floor area legally allowable in this block will in fact be reached. The maximum has greater applicability to small sites, and is not intended as a target for full-block sites having great design flexibility.[21]

Jacobs then proceeded to list seven reasons that the existing Southern Pacific headquarters building should be retained:

> 1. The structure has a richness of detail and materials that cannot be repeated in newer buildings. It is one of the finest representations of the older character of downtown San Francisco that Southern Pacific helped to create.
> 2. The building relates well to the Ferry Building, with which it shares many qualities.
> 3. It is the outstanding element framing the new Embarcadero Plaza, which will become one of the great public spaces of San Francisco.
> 4. It will be complementary to the new Embarcadero Center Hotel, which will present a similar wall to Market Street with a height of 197 feet.
> 5. It constitutes a pleasing end point for the low-level view down California Street, a vista that is increasing in importance as the center of the office district shifts toward lower Market Street.
> 6. The existing building does not take up a significant part of the total floor area . . . and its retention would not inhibit future development in that respect.
> 7. The building presents opportunities, with new development behind it, for a major opening from Market Street through its lobby, and for arcading and retail uses along Market, Spear, and Steuart Streets.[22]

Since Southern Pacific's site was in a critical location relevant to "the city's fabric," Jacobs listed a number of urban design considerations relating to height, bulk, and the general character of the proposed development. He mentioned the following items, stated here in briefer terms:

> 1. California and Pine Streets' view corridors;

2. The need to respect Embarcadero Plaza "in terms of the shadow effects and the total character of new development;"

3. The need for the new structure(s) to be predominantly light in color;

4. The limitation requiring signs to be placed 100 feet above street level; and

5. The relationship of the development to the skyline, bay, and other nearby buildings:

    a. Stepping down of building height as buildings approach the water,

    b. Use of the height of the Ferry Building (235 feet) as a guide for the general range of height appropriate for the site, and

    c. Building towers above a height of 150 to 200 feet not to exceed horizontal dimensions of 170 feet for each building wall and 200 feet for the diagonal measure of the building floor.[23]

Jacobs then indicated that

> There is very little limitation as to the types of uses legally permitted on this site. Economic considerations will undoubtedly determine the uses chosen to a considerable extent. It is likely that a mixture of uses would be found appropriate, although it should be kept in mind that combining more than a few uses in the development could result in greater total height and bulk than might be desired.[24]

Jacobs also stated that proposed parking facilities in excess of 7% of the total building area would be reviewed by the City Planning Commission as a Conditional Use.

Finally, Jacobs stressed that opportunities existed to develop the ground floor level of the new building in a manner which created "new avenues of movement and increased interest for pedestrians."[25] In particular, Jacobs recommended the following urban design considerations:

> 1. The facade of the existing building along Market, Spear and Steuart Streets can be opened up through arcading parallel to the streets and introduction of retail sales and service uses.
>
> 2. One or more passageways can readily be opened from Market Street to the central part of the block, giving additional area for retail. . . . One such possibility would be introduction of a significant open space immediately behind the existing building, with a use such as a garden restaurant. This space might be covered by a transparent roof, provided such a roof would be consistent with the functional aspects of the development.
>
> 3. Parking and loading should be predominantly underground in the development.
>
> 4. Vehicular access to the site would be most feasible on

Spear Street, with Steuart or Mission Street as the second
choice. . . . Care should be taken to avoid conflicts between
vehicles and pedestrians.[26]

On January 28, 1971, the Department of City Planning's urban
designers discussed the status of the Southern Pacific Headquarters site. Very little had been finalized at this point, but concern
was expressed over an economic report conducted by the
Development Research Association in 1969. That report had
advocated that "all-out, mixed-use twin 60-story towers" be
developed on the site, and the urban designers were concerned
that mixed uses "would pile up the floor area."[27]

On February 1, 1971, Passmore sent Jacobs a memorandum
indicating that "we have reviewed urban design and planning code
terms with Welton Becket architects."[28] Passmore reminded Jacobs
to call Hoyt and "emphasize that full use of permitted F. A. R. [was]
not needed on [this] large site to provide ample floor space."[29]

By February 16, 1971, the City Planning Department felt the
following items represented the amount of progress that had
occurred during the design review meeting:

> 1. Southern Pacific wanted to preserve all of the Headquarters
> Building.
> 2. California Street corridor has been preserved, but Pine Street
> had been cut a little.
> 3. Southern Pacific has decided on providing 2 million square
> feet of building space, plus 400,000 square feet from the existing
> building—this was not utilizing the full potential of the site.
> 4. To date, we have tried four different development sites—
> Southern Pacific likes two rectangular buildings, oriented to the
> north of Market grid, including 2 towers, one 20 stories and one 40
> stories. Towers are about 110 feet by 205 feet diagonal—this
> exceeds urban design plan.
> 5. Linde indicated that he may decide this week on how to
> proceed. Mr. Finsterbusch is handling the case now.[30]

After numerous design review meetings, Welton Becket and
Associates submitted six design alternatives for the One Market
Street project to the City Planning Department for review on
March 12, 1971: 1) one tower with 26 floors and approximately
85,000 square feet per floor; 2) one tower with 39 floors with
approximately 63,000 square feet per floor; 3) one tower with 74
floors with approximately 33,000 square feet per floor; 4) one tower
with 64 floors with approximately 39,999 square feet per floor; 5)
two towers—tower one with 25–27 levels at approximately 19,600
square feet, and tower two with 40–42 levels at approximately

40,000 square feet; and 6) two towers—tower one with 25–27 levels at approximately 17,000 square feet, and tower two with 40–42 levels at approximately 19,800 square feet, commercial/office base of six levels at approximately 50,000 square feet.[31]

After the presentation, Jacobs sent a memorandum to Linde and Finsterbusch on March 22, 1971 to relay the Department of City Planning's assessment of the six alternatives. Jacobs stated that

> Of these six alternatives, the first four present extreme difficulties in adaptation to the scale and pattern of the city and to the urban design guidelines used by the Department; these first four schemes also appear to offer fewer opportunities for good internal development of the site.
> Alternatives 5 and 6 are a considerably better scale of development, and although Alternative 5 is designed very specifically to take account of the California and Pine Streets view corridors, we believe that Alternative 6 can accomplish this same purpose and at the same time satisfy the other urban design terms of reference more effectively than Alternative 5. Therefore, the Department favors Alternative 6.[32]

Jacobs then proceeded to discuss Alternative 6 in general terms. The following statements by Jacobs illustrate the major points made in his letter to Linde and Finsterbusch:

> 1. As you know, considerable public sentiment has been expressed for the retention of the California and Pine Street view corridors out to the Bay. We understand that the architects are determining the precise alignment of the view corridors through City surveys.
> 2. As for the size, shape and bulk of the towers, Alternative 6 accomplishes best the condition of stepping down as the buildings approach the water. The inland building (approximately 40 stories) approximates the height of the Pacific Gas & Electric Building further inland, while the tower closer to the water (approximately 25 stories) is a transition to the height of the Ferry Building (18 stories) and to the water. . . . Although a maximum height less than 40 stories in the inland tower might be desirable . . . it is the staff's opinion that a 40-story height in a slender tower is acceptable in order to retain the view corridors and maximize other public potentials in the site.
> 3. We have noted before the building bulk guidelines for the . . . maximum length of a building wall (170 feet) and the maximum horizontal dimension on a diagonal (200 feet). Scheme 6 comes close to meeting these guidelines, and we recommend that the scheme be studied further by the architects to determine whether it can come within the guidelines. It is also important that the two buildings read clearly as separate buildings, and that they have the largest practical gap between them.
> 4. Scheme 6, with its orientation to the south-of-Market grid strengthens the importance of Market Street as the major form

element of downtown . . . and appears to create fewer shadow problems.

    5. The plan for arcading along the streets in the old building . . . is extremely desirable. There is also great potential in the plan for a pedestrian walkway through the block in a north-south direction, with retail uses and an all-weather connection to development further to the south. The possibility of a galleria, open to the roof should be further investigated.

    6. The development of offices is appropriate for the site, especially with considerable retail at ground level.

    7. The plan for a usable rooftop open space on the six-story platform is also commendable. This open space, if kept in sunlight and protected from wind, will produce a major amenity in the project and improve its appearance from nearby buildings.[33]

On March 31, 1971, Welton Becket and Associates sent an Area Summary Sheet to the Department of City Planning and indicated that they selected Alternative 6's design components for their design (see Figs. 12-8 and 12-9). On April 8, 1971, Clifton Brinkley, construction consultant for One Market Plaza, indicated that "the development will conform to *all* our [Department of City Planning] criteria."[34]

Communication among all parties involved in the design review continued, and on May 27, 1971, Jacobs sent a letter of recommendation to the City Planning Commission stating in part:

> Southern Pacific contacted the Department of City Planning last fall, before the start of serious planning for this project. Since that time, communication has been continuous, and the willingness of Southern Pacific and its architects to adhere to urban design terms of reference has been exemplary. . . .
>
> As the architects and Southern Pacific reviewed a number of possible schemes with the Department . . . extremely tall and monolithic towers were rejected, and it became apparent that two towers of smaller size would best meet the design terms. Though the total floor space accommodated in the plans now submitted is imposing, it is far less than the theoretical development potential of the site, and the floor area ratio is only 13.1:1, or less than the 14:1 base ratio allowed *without* bonuses. The floor area is equivalent to what could be built with a base ratio of just 11.1:1 and the present bonuses. It may be observed that Southern Pacific has not set out to build a maximum building.
>
> As the final plans evolved, it was only with considerable difficulty that the architects kept to the three urban design terms affecting the form of the towers: the slope down toward the Bay, the guidelines for horizontal dimensions, and the protection of view corridors. The two towers proposed, at 43 stories on Spear Street and 28 stories on Steuart Street, create a visual effect of sloping toward the Bay. The towers could have been somewhat

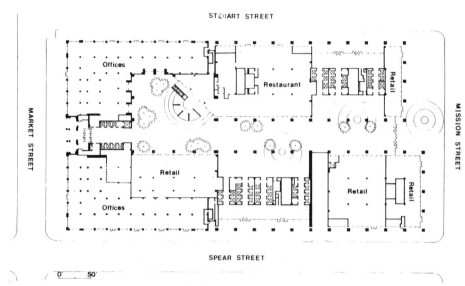

Figure 12-8: One Market Plaza, ground floor plan

Source: One Market Plaza, a Joint Venture of The Equitable Life Assurance Society of the United States and Southern Pacific Land Company.

Figure 12-9: Perspective of One Market Plaza overlooking the San Francisco Bay

Source: One Market Plaza, a Joint Venture of the Equitable Life Assurance Society of the United States and Southern Pacific Land Company.

lower, but then their horizontal dimensions would have been
increased at the expense of . . . the bulk guidelines and view
corridors.[35]

Jacobs did stipulate that if the application for One Market Plaza
were approved, three conditions should be met. First, he stressed
that the staffs of the Department of City Planning and Transit Task
Force should review all exterior ground area designs to ensure that
these elements will be consistent with and complementary to
Market Street. Second, the building facades should be reviewed by
the Department of City Planning, and the proposed towers should
be light in color. Finally, Jacobs felt that the retail area should
provide goods and services for the people working in the general
area and not take shopping facilities from the downtown retail
district.[36]

On May 27, 1971, the City Planning Commission reviewed and
approved the building application for One Market Plaza. The
design review for this project, which lasted approximately nine to
ten months, contributed to producing a building that, in Kenneth
Halpern's opinion,

> represented one of the most compelling arguments that could be
> put forward for the value of urban design controls that can
> integrate the growth of downtown areas with the best features of
> its past developments. The buildings may not be a triumph of
> architectural design, according to conventional aesthetic criteria;
> but this is more a problem with the state of architectural criticism
> than it is a problem with this particular building. The urban design
> controls have prevented a building that, if built conventionally,
> would have been conspicuous and brutal on San Francisco's
> delicate landscape, no matter how sophisticated in traditional
> design terms. By conforming to the urban design controls, the
> building has become a piece of "background" architecture that
> functions as well as any new office building but maintains a
> respect for more important surrounding environmental qualities.[37]

Overall, One Market Plaza can be considered a successful and
useful building, from both a functional and aesthetic point of view
(see Figs. 12-10 to 12-13). Southern Pacific Company and its
architects were successful in designing One Market Plaza so that it
did not appear bulky. The difference in height between the two
buildings—one 43 stories and the second 28 stories—helped to
distinguish the buildings as being separate from each other.
Furthermore, the 45 feet of space left between the two towers and
the fact that the two towers were thin also helped to eliminate a
bulky appearance.

Figure 12-10: One Market Plaza, the galleria's climate-controlled environment provides a pleasant atmosphere for retail shops

Figure 12-11: One Market Plaza, through-block mall provides pleasant indoor access to next block

Figure 12-12: One Market Plaza, Restaurant located in the mall for further amenity

Figure 12-13: One Market Plaza, overall view

The plaza of One Market Plaza is located in the south side of the building; thus, the plaza should receive sufficient sunlight during the day. But, the "seating capacity, landscaping, other amenities, and overall design of this plaza are not outstanding."[38] The lack of apparent use of the plaza may be attributed to the fact that there is little activity beyond Mission Street and that the through-block plaza does not lead anywhere. In the near future, however, when new developments are built in the area and in particular after the preservation of buildings across from Mission Street is finished, the plaza will likely become more active and useful. Other than this problem with the building, One Market Plaza is quite successful.

The developers and architects of the One Market Plaza complex had a good working relationship with the Department of City Planning. A number of factors may have contributed to this working relationship. First, Southern Pacific Company demonstrated to the Department of City Planning as early as 1967 they were interested in developing the Market Street Block site by meeting with personnel of the Department and asking for the city's urban design criteria. Again in 1968 there was interaction between the Southern Pacific Company and the urban designers of the Department of City Planning which further illustrated Southern Pacific's desire to work cooperatively with the city. Jacobs seemed to be impressed with Southern Pacific Company's efforts to communicate with the Department of City Planning: in a memorandum to the City Planning Commission on May 27, 1971, Jacobs made certain that the Commissioners were aware of Southern Pacific's cooperative attitude.

The fact that the Southern Pacific Company was a long-term resident of San Francisco also seemed to have the effect of encouraging the Company to build a complex which would complement its surroundings. A San Francisco newspaper article dated March 8, 1971, quoted Linde as saying

> Southern Pacific has been in San Francisco for almost 100 years and in its present building since 1917, and we are well aware of the great beauty and charm of San Francisco.
>   We have been in close contact with the City Planning Director and his staff in an effort to develop a plan which would enhance the City's skyline and complement the adjacent Embarcadero Plaza at the foot of Market Street.[39]

There is also evidence that the Department of City Planning, as well as the City Planning Commission, wanted a congenial working relationship. A Department of City Planning interoffice memorandum written by one of the members of the design review team for One Market Plaza indicated: "ABJ [Allan B. Jacobs] stressed cooperation, and desire of the City Planning Commission to be informed" of the One Market Plaza Project.[40] This is further substantiated in Jacobs' May 27, 1971 memorandum to the City Planning Commission:

> In the plan proposed, the greatest horizontal wall dimension is 175 feet and the greatest diagonal dimension is 209 feet. The excess of five feet along the wall and nine feet in the diagonal of the larger tower [the Urban Design Plan guidelines state wall and diagonal dimensions of a maximum of 170 feet and 200 feet respectively] is felt by the Department to be reasonable in view of the other design terms that have been imposed.[41]

The above paragraph illustrates that the Department of City Planning and the Southern Pacific Company had a give-and-take type of relationship. Jacobs apparently thought the Department could afford to compromise on certain design issues to a minimum degree in exchange for other design issues that were felt to be more important in One Market Plaza's design. For instance, Southern Pacific expressed an initial desire to demolish the Southern Pacific Headquarters but reconsidered its earlier position and decided to include the headquarters in the proposed building. It is quite possible that the Southern Pacific Company changed its mind after receiving a memorandum from Jacobs which listed seven reasons for keeping the building (as previously cited). Southern Pacific may not have been aware of the advantages of retaining the building until the Department of City Planning pointed them out; perhaps it did not know that the Department of City Planning wanted Southern Pacific to retain the building. The fact that the urban designers of the Department of City Planning explicitly stated design terms they wanted included in the proposed development at the very beginning of design review helped to eliminate any misconception on the part of the Southern Pacific Company. Furthermore, there then was no need for Southern Pacific to submit plans which purposely "tested" the position of the Department of City Planning.

The overall decision-making environment in San Francisco also tended to reinforce the cooperative attitude of the Southern Pacific

Company; in particular, the Southern Pacific Company knew that the Department of City Planning and the City Planning Commission were strongly supported by citizens of San Francisco. Thus, Southern Pacific's agreeable behavior was more or less a form of self-protection, and Southern Pacific was prepared to accept only design terms which were stated in the urban design guidelines. If the City Planning Commission and the Department of City Planning would have approved a more economically desirable scheme for One Market Plaza, Southern Pacific knew that various citizens groups against high-rise buildings, such as San Francisco Tomorrow, would have voiced their disapproval of the building and would likely have interfered with the planning process. This circumstance clearly illustrates the fact that various citizen interest groups have clout within San Francisco's political framework which serves to strengthen the Department of City Planning's position. Even though political power placed in the hands of citizen groups tends to make it more difficult for urban designers to deal with design issues strictly on a professional level, citizen groups in San Francisco provide necessary backup and power to help the city's urban designers get the type of buildings that are most desired by both city officials and the public.

Overall, design review had a positive impact on the planning process of the One Market Plaza project. That the Urban Design Plan guidelines were specific on design issues the city felt were absolutely crucial, such as protection of view corridors, served a useful purpose. The written guidelines established the credibility of San Francisco's urban design criteria and also assured developers that the criteria would apply to all proposed developments in San Francisco. Further, the guidelines limited the discretionary power that the urban designers of the Department of City Planning could exercise on these specific issues; yet they also gave the urban designers some limited flexibility to negotiate certain design terms. In the One Market Plaza case, the urban designers accepted the proposed development even though the building mass was slightly over the maximum limits stated in the Urban Design Plan.

Adding to the effectiveness of the design review in San Francisco was the fact that the Director of City Planning was an urban designer. Jacobs's training, experience, and sensitivity to urban design issues enabled him to organize and run a productive design review effectively. Moreover, his ability to distinguish between important and unimportant design terms and to put them in proper perspective enabled the urban designers to keep the design review segment of the planning process relatively short. Certainly, design review did not bog down with a multitude of picayune issues.

Notes

1. Kenneth Halpern (1978). *Downtown USA: Urban Design in Nine American Cities* (New York: Whitney Library of Design), pp. 162–163.

2. Thomas Cooke (1976). "A Process for Community Design," *Practicing Planner,* 6: 30.

3. Halpern (1978), p. 163.

4. Allan B. Jacobs (1978). *Making City Planning Work.* (Chicago: ASPO Publications), pp. 227–228.

5. Paul Van Slambrouck (1975). "Things are looking up at One Market Plaza," *San Francisco Business,* April: 13–14.

6. San Francisco Department of City Planning (1971a). *Memorandum* from A. B. Jacobs to the City Planning Commission, "Discretionary Review of Building Application No. 396943 for Southern Pacific Headquarters Block (One Market Plaza)," May 27, p. 3.

7. *Ibid.,* pp. 1–2.

8. Van Slambrouck (1975), 14–16.; and "Pipestruts Clear Way for Building Excavation" (1974), *ENR,* August 1, p. 22.

9. San Francisco City Planning Commission (1971). Resolution No. 6111, May 27.

10. San Francisco Department of City Planning (1967). *Memorandum,* February 14, p. 1.

11. San Francisco Department of City Planning (1971a), p. 1.

12. "Southern Pacific Mixes High Rise Building" (1971). *San Francisco Bay Guardian,* March 8.

13. San Francisco Department of City Planning (1971a), p. 3.

14. "Southern Pacific Mixes High Rise Building" (1971), *ibid.*

15. Van Slambrouck (1975), p. 15.

16. "Pipestruts Clear Way for Building Excavation" (1974), p. 22.

17. San Francisco Department of City Planning (1970a). *Memorandum* from A. B. Jacobs to the file, November 19, p. 1.

18. San Francisco Department of City Planning (n.d.). *Memorandum* from Dewayne Guyer to Richard Hedman and Peter Svirsky, "Design Terms of Reference for Southern Pacific Market Street Headquarters," p. 1.

19. San Francisco Department of City Planning (1970*b*). Letter from A. B. Jacobs to L. E. Hoyt, Vice President of Southern Pacific Company, "Southern Pacific Headquarters Block," December 11, p. 1.

20. *Ibid.*, p. 2.

21. *Ibid.*

22. *Ibid.*, pp. 2–3.

23. *Ibid.*, pp. 3–4.

24. *Ibid.*, p. 4.

25. *Ibid.*

26. *Ibid.*, pp. 4–5.

27. San Francisco Department of City Planning (1970*c*). *Memorandum*, January 28, p.1.

28. San Francisco Department of City Planning (1971*b*). *Memorandum* from R. Passmore to A. B. Jacobs, "Southern Pacific Headquarters Block," February 1, p. 1.

29. *Ibid.*, pp. 1–2.

30. San Francisco Department of City Planning (1971). *Memorandum*, February 16, p. 1.

31. Welton, Becket, and Associates (1971). Letter to the City Planning Department, "One Market Street Project," March 12, pp. 1–2.

32. San Francisco Department of City Planning (1971*c*). *Memorandum* from A. B. Jacobs to O. G. Linde and W. A. Finsterbusch, "Southern Pacific Headquarters Block," March 22, p. 1.

33. *Ibid.*, pp. 2–4.

34. San Francisco Department of City Planning (1971*d*). *Memorandum*, April 7, p. 1.

35. San Francisco Department of City Planning (1971*a*), pp. 1–3.

36. *Ibid.*, p. 3.

37. Halpern (1978), p. 161.

38. Ann Quist Skaff (1978). "The San Francisco Urban Design Plan: Goals, Implementation, and Resulting Development in the Downtown," M.C.P. thesis, University of California, Berkeley, p. 169.

39. "Southern Pacific Mixes High Rise Building" (1971), *ibid.*

40. San Francisco Department of City Planning (1971*e*). *Memorandum*, March 1, p. 1.

41. San Francisco Department of City Planning (1971*a*), p. 2.

Part IV

Findings and Recommendations

13
Findings

A Brief Review

We have been investigating the process of design review in city governments in order to examine the effectiveness of specific models of present review process, to explore relationships between model features and the environments in which they operate, and to draw conclusions about the ways in which models for design review can be organized in differing environmental situations. More specifically, the purpose of this study has been to do the following: 1) introduce the urban design review process; 2) study four different processes of urban design review; 3) explore four case studies to illustrate how our design review process works; and 4) offer recommendations for improvements to the design review process and for cities wishing to establish a design review process.

To facilitate comparison of the four methods of design review, diagrams showing the approach, nature, elements, and management have been designated for each city (see Figs. 7-1 to 7-4). The themes common to the models as well as their differentiated features have then been identified. I have placed emphasis on the characteristics of the models themselves rather than on the characteristics of the environments in which they function. After each model was analyzed, I developed a comparative study and classification.

Chapters 9–12 examined the urban design review process with a specific case study in each city: Boston, the Charleston Savings Bank project; Minneapolis, The Crossing; New York City, Olympic Tower; and San Francisco, One Market Plaza. Many illustrations and drawings have further allowed comparisons among the case studies. With details of the case studies freshly in mind, I provided an analysis of and observations on the studies; the inner workings of the design review process in each case were thereby revealed.

This chapter includes a discussion of the environmental factors that influence design review for the citizens, the city, the developer, and the architect. Among them are the extent of political and financial support for the process, the importance of citizen input, and the qualifications which the review members bring to their deliberations.

General Observations from the Cases: Environmental Factors

One can conclude that there are a number of factors within the city environment that influence the choice of a specific model to match the environment. These factors are not common to all the models studied here. The differences among the four city environments make some factors applicable to all, while others are applicable only to one, two, or three of the cities. These factors also have a high interdependency with each other. In the following discussion, pertinent factors will be identified by re-examination and comparison of the cases. Although this study has looked at four cities, it is quite evident other cities may find themselves in a similar situation.

Level of Political Support

Undoubtedly, political support from the chief executive and the policy-makers is a crucial factor in the creation and establishment of the urban design function as well as the design review process within a city government. Lu has stated that an effective "urban design office has direct lines of communication with the chief executive and policy-makers of the city (mayor, city council, or city manager)."[1] Yet, the extent of political support is a very complicated subject and can result in varying effects on the design review process. Results of the four case studies indicate that a moderate amount of political support is desirable. Indeed, greater political support may be counterproductive; conversely, lesser political support often brings inefficiency, and the design review may become slow and cumbersome as well.

In the Boston case, it appears that despite political support being high, the quality of urban design and expertise needed for the design review process is diminishing. In the Charleston Savings Bank project, the architect and developer were correct in their assessment that they had to wait too long for approval of their project. Again, they were correct in pointing out that all the power to accept or reject the proposal was in the hands of a single person, Sloan. Boston's system, intended to encourage design review sessions to take place, faltered in the Charleston Savings Bank case in that Sloan's personal opinion ruled on a design detail, not on a bigger issue of form and massing. Clearly, the BRA needs written guidelines for design review to avoid controversy. Sloan might have been "right" in his approach to the Charleston Savings Bank project, but there is no assurance that in other cities, or in different cases, other urban designers will be "right," too—that they will not use their discretionary powers because of their own self-interests.

The present situation in New York City indicates diminishing political support. Mayor Koch, in an economic crunch, has sacrificed the Office of Midtown Planning and Development.[2] Although the establishment of OMPD was a major attempt to implement urban design at the district level during Mayor Lindsay's administration, the present level of political support for urban design functions is very minimal, with almost no money available for such activity.[3] Minneapolis and San Francisco both enjoy moderate political support for urban design as is quite evident from the case discussions. Their successes, however, were not wholly dependent upon moderate political support from the city officials; other environmental factors were of influence as well.

Availability of Resources

The resources a city can devote to incorporating the urban design function into its administration and to establishing a design review process also play a crucial role. All the cities studied here devoted a moderate or high level of resources to this activity. Minneapolis seems to have quite adequate support for design review in the near future. San Francisco to a higher degree and Boston to a lesser degree are having funding problems. In Boston this is caused by depletion of urban renewal monies and in San Francisco, by cutbacks in the budget. Consequently, for the past two years BRA has not had a Director of its Urban Design Department, and the number of staff members has dropped from 14 to 11, leaving mostly senior members. In San Francisco the Department of City Planning's Director, Rai Okamoto, says his department has had serious financial problems.[4] This in turn has resulted in a reduction of the size of the planning and urban design staff.

The New York City case is quite different from the others. New York City, even during the Lindsay administration and the establishment of FASD and other special districts, had a moderate level of resources available. Presently, the level is very minimal with almost no money available for such activity. True, FASD and other special districts are established by city zoning ordinances and lack of funds will not change their existence; but the reduction of staff has a direct effect on the amount of work that can be accomplished and therefore does adversely affect the urban design function. A moderate level of resources is, then, necessary to establish and maintain the design review process. The efficiency of design review does not necessarily go up as the level of resources increases, for then other factors may come into play. For example, the review mechanism has to be carefully drawn for due process and equal protection for developers, architects, and the public, lest the process become cumbersome with repeated lawsuits.[5]

Level of Concern by Public Officials

With reasonable political support and an adequate level of resources, a city still may have no procedure to implement urban design even when this procedure is present. Indeed, there may be no efficient design review model with a full range of components, for its efficiency depends on the level of concern manifested for urban design by the executive decision-making body. All four cities studied here have had a high interest in urban design. In addition, Minneapolis officials have made an effort to create an atmosphere where the public and private sectors can work more effectively together. Presently, the same level of interest and concern about urban design exists in the cities of Boston, Minneapolis, and San Francisco. In New York City recently, however, officials have much less interest and concern.

Citizen Support and Involvement

Citizens can play an important role and can influence the choice of the design review procedure. Indeed, citizen acceptance of the idea of design review is basic to establishment of the procedure. Written criteria and guidelines for the design review can increase its palatability to the public. Another pitfall that may need to be overcome is citizen apprehension that design review may be misused as a means of perpetuating exclusiveness or exclusion,[6] which, of course, has happened. Citizens may be persuaded to accept design review as a means of controlling physical change which in itself may be threatening. Jacobs adds, however, that

> It is not always understood by those concerned with the visual and sensory relationships between people and their environment, especially by those offended by the design quality of new development, that city planning departments are rarely responsible for the direct design of anything.[7]

The citizens need to know this. Lindbloom offers additional suggestions on winning citizen support.[8] He certainly is optimistic when he says that "all it takes is desire" for a city that wants to establish environmental design review.[9] At the basic level, homogeneity and heterogeneity of the residents within a city or area strongly affect choices of a model for design review. In Minneapolis, for example, homogeneity makes it easier to define "good" urban design, to find something that a majority of people are agreed upon, and to develop a high sense of cooperation. Recall, however, that Minneapolis may have evidenced some citizen apathy.

It is not easy to get citizen participation in government, let alone in planning and urban design matters. Sometimes, however, they rise to the occasion. Professionals, architects in this case, recognized their civic responsibilities: The New York City Chapter of AIA in 1964 formed the first CDC (community design center) called ARCH (Architects Renewal Committee in Harlem) to aid in combatting "improvements like a freeway." By 1976 there were 80 such CDCs, and they became advocacy groups providing professional and technical support and design assistance. A former architectural director of the Philadelphia workshop said:

> Of long range advantage to professionals is the fact that CDCs have introduced low-income people to the practical benefits of good architecture and planning. . . . As time has passed we've

learned to concentrate on being educators instead of spokesmen.[10]

Applebaum feels that the Santa Barbara Planning Task Force did a better job than in many cities in gaining citizen support and involvement for a study on impacts of growth in the city:

> The task force succeeded in involving far larger numbers of people in all phases of its work than other comparable studies with which I am familiar. Nor was involvement limited to university students. . . . The response to the study far exceeded the customary yawn given to most such reports. There is a long-standing historical tradition of citizen apathy in our communities, which is currently abetted by a widespread mistrust of anything having to do with government. In light of these conditions, the task force could well be judged a successful initial step towards reinvolving people at a grass-roots level in those complex issues that will ultimately shape their future.[11]

New York City's heterogeneity of cultures and people from various parts of the world and with totally different backgrounds makes it extremely difficult to come to an agreement on what is "good" urban design, to gain cooperation, and to have support from all members of the society. In such a situation, it is easier to gain support for design in a specific area or neighborhood rather than in the entire city.

The citizens' involvement, historical character, and overall level of education are also quite important to the success of urban design review. In San Francisco, one of the strongest assets is highly active citizen groups. On the other hand, Boston's historical and architectural character focuses the attention of people and the city administration toward the subject of the urban design function. The greater the citizen support, the stronger are the positions of the urban designers and planners of the city. However, too much citizen support and strength may bring conflict between the professional opinions and the people's ideas. For example, citizens of San Francisco do not like high-rise buildings, but this does not necessarily mean that a high-rise building is inappropriate in the downtown area. Therefore, exactly as in the case of too much political support or too much discretion in the hands of the review members, too much citizen support and involvement may be counterproductive.

Yet it is important to have faith in the constituency of a city, "members of communities with proud traditions of home rule. Put a well thought out action program before these people and they'll be willing to pay for it."[12] Lu describes "effective public involvement in the urban design process" as:

> Perhaps the single most important element in a successful urban design program in local government. . . . Public attitudes form the context within which design must be implemented, and so these attitudes have a profound influence on the environmental quality a city develops. In addition, it is the public, or "consumers" of urban design, who often have the most to teach designers about specific environmental problems or situations. Those actually involved in the situation often have the most detailed information and the most useful ideas for improvements.[13]

However, there has to be a mechanism for citizen involvement, a way for them to express opinion on the establishment of urban design elements, on the nature of those elements, and on guidelines. San Francisco, among the four cities studied here, was most efficient in having an urban design plan which was formulated with a significant amount of citizen input. This plan enables San Francisco to provide the amenities that the citizens desire. Furthermore, this plan prescribes a hearing process which gives the opportunity for further citizen input on specific proposed projects. The other cities lacked such a mechanism, although they do have some citizen input.

Public hearings in which the whole community participates may not be an adequate means of promoting community involvement. Frequently, people do not attend public hearings because they are frustrated at what seems to be a useless process which is more political than anything else. In order to have community input, one first has to educate citizens about urban design issues and then ask for their viewpoints. The City of Tucson, Arizona, uses a productive method to achieve citizen input. A questionnaire with a detailed explanation of the proposed project (including photographs and sketches) is mailed to the citizens. Their opinions on the project are used to establish guidelines.[14] It is important to structure appropriate public participation in the review process and give the public "the tools to shape and influence public policy [so that they may] articulate their ideas and desires with regard to specific and general issues."[15] Appleyard has suggested several ways to elicit citizen opinion: selected sampling, mail-back questionnaires, surveys, telephone interviews, etc.[16] The applicability of these methods in practice may be questionable. Indeed, not everyone thinks that citizen participation is an asset. In

describing citizen participation in a study of revitalization of the
Hollywood section of Los Angeles, Freeman was quite blunt:

> Those involved [the professionals, that is] foresaw some of the
> pitfalls of local people doing the study—possible charges of vested
> interests, dissatisfaction by local people who would not participate,
> etc.—and tried to minimize them.[17]

Market Pressures

The nature of the market in a city or in an area of a city is a factor
which directly affects the nature of the urban development. The
more effective the control of urban physical development, the
better its quality will be. Therefore, when an area is undergoing a
major development boom, great consideration should be given to
the design review model and its components: approach, nature,
and elements. In Minneapolis, officials saw the city deteriorating;
urban development was therefore encouraged in an effort to keep
people in the city. The heavy market pressures that caused New
York City to adopt the FASD regulations have continued.
Developers are eager to build there in preference to many locations
in the other boroughs. Controversy continues over the efficacy of
FASD guidelines to deal with these pressures. Most recently,
Trump Tower has come under fire.[18]

However, a city should adopt an urban design procedure only
after careful deliberation and study of the economic, social, and
political characteristics of a city (or part of a city). I have already
stated that I do not feel that New York City and its citizens get as
much return from incentive zoning as the developers do. Recall,
too, that in New York City the FASD does not contain penalties for
not following the approved plans, certainly a flaw in a successful
urban design review process. The four cities studied here are all
under high market pressure for development.

Qualifications of Design Review Members

Design review members play an important role in creating a
successful environment for review, compromise, and negotiation.
At minimum, they have the highest responsibility for educating
the public concerning what urban design can do and how it can
improve the environmental quality of the city. Santa Barbara,

California, for example, developed a Neighborhood Fact Book to educate the citizenry to the unique features of the 33 neighborhoods in the city. Included were analyses of the impacts of growth on each neighborhood.[19]

Reviewers should also be capable of understanding the developer's needs and wants as well as his architect's desire to have freedom of creativity. Therefore, the reviewers' attitude, personality, responsiveness, and qualifications are all of extreme importance. The time that the review body consumes in its deliberations and the level of discretion exercised by a reviewer also are important and strongly influence the other factors in the review process.

Because the reviewers hold the central position in the design review process, it is useful to examine the kinds of skills they use in order to be effective. There are basically two general types of expertise that a successful reviewer must have—technical and political. The technical skills needed are based on the reviewer's knowledge of urban design. It should be obvious that the reviewer must have a thorough understanding of urban design in order to determine accurately the feasibility of specific design elements.

A professional architect or planner does not automatically qualify as an urban designer. However, an AIA study of design review boards reveals that 97% of the boards that answered their 1974 survey were architects.[20] Although several review members should definitely have expertise in such fields as economics, law, transportation, and so on, it is the basic knowledge of urban design which is needed for a design review member. Urban designers can always call in experts in other fields for their opinion on the issues that they cannot easily analyze.

The main role of such a design review member, an urban designer, should be to help the public obtain what they want and should not center on his professional opinion alone. Urban designers must use their professional expertise to understand the public and attempt to inform them in the best possible way. An urban designer, like a city's planning professionals, is caught in the middle between the developer, his architect, the city administration, and lastly, the public. He is buffeted from all sides and pleases no one. A "thick skin" is probably a desirable attribute for urban designers.[21]

Domination by architects with no understanding of urban

design in the review process will cause urban design to be large-scale architecture and "form-making."

> An urban design plan is not a prescription for bricks and mortar
> but rather a set of framing and constraining prescriptions from
> which architects, landscape architects and engineers can design
> and build. . . . Urban designers may never design a specific
> building or buildings embodied in an urban plan, but rather lay the
> ground rules for the professions involved with construction.[22]

In the extreme, the sole issues might become "aesthetic" and the criteria, primarily subjective.

The political skills needed by an effective design reviewer revolve around a basic understanding of the decision-making process, including the role of interest group coalitions, so as to anticipate accurately sources of opposition and support and to enhance the legitimacy and effectiveness of his or her own position. In addition, a reviewer needs a strong sense of self-assurance and the ability to compromise when necessary.

Negotiating is the activity common to nearly all discretionary review processes. Whether it is the ability to form a covert conspiracy with an architect who shares the same opinions of good design or a skill at "horse-trading" favors for amenities, a successful reviewer must know how to "play the game." He must understand that design trade-offs may be so expensive for a developer that he will be pushed into going over the reviewer's head to higher political authority. Likewise, the cost of delay may be as real as the cost of providing an amenity, and the revenues lost as a result of eliminating a few square feet of rentable office space per floor is certain to affect the complexion of the developer's balance sheet.[23]

Powell, a developer of Governor's Square in Sacramento, California, has advice for other developers: "What a private developer must consider is whether the additional costs can be compensated by increased marketability." As an example, he uses asphalt: "not the formula for aesthetic effect, nor is it likely to bring people trooping in from suburbs." He further states that landscape alone is not the answer to financial or aesthetic success. "Other factors . . . are the environment or the larger area where the project is situated, overall design of the complex."[24]

In dealing with architects, the reviewer faces a different relationship than the one he has with developers. A reviewer can choose to play the role of "regulator"—a stubborn defender of the public interest, unwilling to compromise on any essential point. Alternatively, a reviewer may decide to work with the architect as a "joint learner," assuming, of course, that the latter is so inclined. Each participant has to respect the skills and opinions of the other as they both search for the best solution to a particular design problem. In the first instance, an adversary relationship can emerge which may make the smallest concession a matter of pride. Each side may stubbornly maintain its position until only the force of power can effectively intervene. In the second case, urban design becomes a cooperative effort in which two professionals share their insight into a problem and set aside egos and ambitions for the good of the process.[25]

Neither approach is appropriate in all situations. Any series of sessions will likely require a discretionary assessment of the value of stubbornness over compromise and vice versa. The sensitivity that a reviewer needs for such assessment comes partially from experience but also from basic principles that have been personally formulated.[26] Perhaps what is needed is that function of urban design enabling successful adaptation to a particular urban environment.

> Professionals should be able to take up the issues of how
> instinctively they speak for the particular client group, and how
> much they can let their own personal intuitions play without
> violating the sense of purpose of the specific culture in which they
> find themselves.[27]

All of the preceding information on reviewers applies to the proper use of professionals on review boards. However, in many cities the law provides for appointed boards. The situation then changes. There may be prejudice against professionals' serving on such a board. (Cook warns that experts may insert their prejudices into the review.)[28] Opposition may also be strong to the appointment of persons with real estate connections. In such cities, then, there may be a severe lack of expertise. For the sake of his/her own preservation, the planning professional who is employed by the city has a large education problem to solve. Cities, like individuals, get caught up in enthusiasms and may espouse urban design review without making sufficient preparations. The planning professional had better help the city make review successful. Cook states a definite preference for review by a

professional staff[29] rather than by an appointed board; such a
choice may not be available in some cities.

Clarity of Goals and Objectives

To avoid conflicts, design criteria and guidelines should become
regulative as much as possible, but they should allow for a certain
level of discretion by concentrating on the appropriateness of the
alternatives in a proposed development. The developer's interest is
naturally financial. Design review should be responsive and
satisfying to the developer whose most critical factor is time. Hillis
and Friedman report horror stories of time lost by developers
because of the state of Washington's multi-layered regulations
(remedied somewhat by ECPA coordinated permit procedures).
They suggest what some would consider unrealistic—subsidiza-
tion of "developments directed at achieving public goals." They
also ask that "rather than aiming at demonstration projects, they
[public efforts] should be aimed at changing the incentive
structures of development and distributing the incentives to all
developments meeting established criteria."[30]

Therefore, the city should explain in advance exactly what it
wants, try to be reasonable, and realize the developer's needs. The
developer should have the specific criteria for urban design
available to him before his design is presented for initial review.
Procedures in Minneapolis, New York City, and San Francisco are
quite reasonable and productive in this respect. Successful design
review must definitely relate to the overall urban design and
planning process of the city. For example, San Francisco's design
review process is more successful than in the three other cities
because it is part of a larger urban policy.

Options Open to the Developer

One of the other important factors which affects the design revie'
process is the extent of the options open to the developer. In the
case of Boston, the developer has almost no options except those
specified by the design review members. Minneapolis, New York
City, and San Francisco were much more flexible in this regard; in
particular, New York City has a well-organized option system that
allows choices to the developer, but this is partly due to the
incentive zoning mechanism and bonus system.

"Atlanta has enjoyed a creative partnership between local government and the business community that has raised Atlanta from regional to national stature."[31] "An accidental city with a laissez-faire approach to planning," Dunlop explains, "Atlanta has placed great faith in the good will, good judgement, and good intentions of its downtown developers. For the most part this faith has been rewarded . . . with public amenities in profusion."[32]

Examples are given. Though no sizable open space was provided by developers, private funds totalling $13 million were donated to correct this. In 1975 Atlanta's new charter took effect and established a strong planning department. Atlanta now is following one of the important precepts of good urban design by developing a comprehensive plan to use MARTA, the transit system, "to enhance the city."[33]

Freedom for Creativity and Innovation

Equally important is the level of freedom allowed to the architect or designer for creativity and innovation. In the case of Boston, the level of freedom was quite minimal. At the other extreme in San Francisco, a sufficient level of freedom was provided for the architect; in addition, design review members showed their sensitivity and assisted the architect by spelling out the urban design plan guidelines, thereby ensuring a better product.

Outside Ranks of Influence

The extent of influence from outside the design review process may be very important in changing the decisions within that process. As is clear in the case of Boston, the review member as well as the developer attempted to bring outside influences to bear. In the three other cases, such routes of modification were not significantly used. Design review members must keep this possibility clearly in mind.

Extent and Scope of Elements

The extent and scope of urban design elements reviewed in the process center on either aesthetic or functional issues or both. In Minneapolis and New York City, there was concentration on functional issues; in Boston emphasis was on aesthetic concerns

more than in the three other cities. The only city in our study
which completely examined both functional and aesthetic issues
was San Francisco. The town of Brookline, Massachusetts, has
prepared two booklets to guide developers through that town's
environmental review process. Illustrations are effectively used to
indicate both aesthetic principles (trees, flowers, harmony with
other buildings, and so on) and functional design (minimizing
shade on other buildings, access, and so on).[34]

Overall Level of Planning Activities

Overall urban planning activities, research, and analysis in regard
to urban development carry an important weight in the design
review process. The fact that San Francisco and Minneapolis have a
high level of overall planning activities and a significant amount of
published and updated materials in regard to urban development
and objectives greatly aids the design review process in these
cities.[35] San Francisco is a unique and ideal case to study since the
city has an urban design plan which exactly specifies the
guidelines, elements to be reviewed, and the overall goals and
objectives of the public in regard to the city's environmental
quality.

Level of Public—Private Cooperation

The level of cooperation between the public and the private sector
also affects the design review process. In Minneapolis, for
example, we have observed how significant this influence was in
the urban design and planning processes and therefore in the
design review process. San Francisco, to some extent, has
maintained some degree of such cooperation; however, the other
two cities discussed in this study lack this factor.

Effectiveness of Bureaucratic Organization

How well a planning department and/or urban design body is
organized with accurate records of past projects facilitates examination of previous and similar projects and therefore enables
application of the lessons learned from these projects. The size of
the city's bureaucracy is an influential factor in the design review

process, too. As we have observed, one of the problems in New York City has been its huge bureaucracy. So many city agencies are involved in the planning process that design review becomes time consuming. Next to New York City, San Francisco has extensive problems; but cities like Boston and Minneapolis, with a smaller scope for their urban design activities, do not have such a problem.

Size of City Bureaucracy

Clark states that Seattle, one of the first U.S. cities to have a design commission, has a bureaucracy problem. However, he tries to put this problem in perspective:

> The concerns of the commission about better design and improved environments sometimes run counter to the ideas of departmental chiefs about the budgets for and the program descriptions of the particular project. . . . Since the commission is advisory and the director of the department of community development is not always on an equal footing with other departmental directors, the commission's recommendations are occasionally (whether intentionally or not) subverted.[36]

Level of Cooperation

Not only is the size of the bureaucracy important, but also the level of cooperation between the various city agencies is very crucial and might have a positive or negative effect on the design review process. Some of the problems with the FASD in New York City were created by the lack of cooperation among various city agencies. On the other hand, one of the positive aspects of the Minneapolis and San Francisco cases was well organized and cooperative efforts among city agencies. This factor does not apply completely to Boston because of the existence of BRA, an accomplished merger of various agencies (planning commission, planning department, urban design body, etc.).

Overlapping of Responsibility

Overlapping of responsibility given to various agencies can complicate the design review and has a direct effect on the developer and his architect. For example, San Francisco is beginning to face such a problem by having established an office of

environmental review separate from the city's planning department which already dealt with these problems. There are also
problems in gaining cooperation among the agencies at various
levels of government.

Okamoto and Williams' comments on the problems that may
develop between the public and the private sectors and among city
agencies are most appropriate:

> Clearly, therefore, well-designed business districts with good
> access to buildings from subways and a better environment for the
> pedestrian generally will not be carried out with business-and-
> government-as-usual. . . . These 'paper' walls between agencies,
> both public and private, result in real walls detouring subway
> riders from their destinations, blocking pedestrians from light and
> air and cutting meaningful open space into a patchwork.[37]

Length of Review Process

Finally, one of the most important factors is the time required to
complete the design review process. Lengthy procedures make the
work of the developer and his architect cumbersome. The cost of
delay and the resultant loss of competitive edge may be as great as
the cost of providing a public amenity.[38] Boston and Minneapolis
have substantially lower time frames for design review than New
York City or San Francisco.

To summarize, the influential environmental factors in the
design review process are the following:

1. Level of political support.
2. Availability of resources.
3. Level of concern by public officials.
4. Citizen support and involvement.
5. Market pressures.
6. Qualifications of the design review members.
7. Clarity of goals and objectives.
8. Options open to the developer.
9. Freedom for creativity and innovation.
10. Outside routes of influence.
11. Extent and scope of elements.
12. Overall level of planning activity.
13. Level of public-private cooperation.
14. Effectiveness of bureaucratic organization.
15. Size of city bureaucracy.

16. Level of cooperation.
17. Overlapping of responsibility.
18. Length of review process.

Notes

1. Weiming Lu (1976). *Urban Design Role in Local Government* (Dallas: Dallas Department of Urban Planning), p. 16

2. Glenn Fowler (1980). "Planning Agency Breaks Up Urban Design Group," *The New York Times*, March 28: Section A, p. 26.

3. Jacquelin Robertson (1980). Personal conversation, June 19.

4. Rai Okamoto (1980). Speech during the APA National Planning Conference in San Francisco, April 12–16.

5. The American Institute of Architects (AIA) Committee on Design (1974). *Design Review Boards: A Handbook for Communities* (Washington: American Institute of Architects), p. 10.

6. *Ibid.*

7. Allan Jacobs (1978). *Making City Planning Work* (Chicago: American Society of Planning Officials), pp. 192–193.

8. Carl G. Lindbloom (1970). *Environmental Design Review* (West Trenton, N.J.: Chandler-Davis Publishing), pp. 19–24.

9. *Ibid.*, p. 36

10. Andrea O. Dean (1976). "Community Design Centers: Practicing 'Social Architecture'," *AIA Journal*, 65: 38–41.

11. Richard P. Applebaum (1976). "Natural for Whom? Studying Growth in Santa Barbara," *Environmental Comment*, February, p. 7.

12. Allan Jacobs (1978). "Jacobs: Planners, Plan Thy Own Cities!" *APA News*, June, p. 5.

13. Lu (1976), p. 3.

14. Tucson Department of Planning (n.d.). "Tucson Urban Design."

15. Lu (1976), p. 4.

16. Donald Appleyard (1977). "Need Analyses Aid Priority Setting," *Practicing Planner*, 7: 31–34.

17. Allen Freeman (1976). "A Local AIA Urban Design Team Helps the Nation's Former Glamor Capital Attempt a Comeback," *AIA Journal*, 65: 76.

18. News Report (1979). "Retail Construction: Wholesale Destruction." *Progressive Architecture*, July, p. 25; and Howard Blum (1980). "Trump: The Development of a Manhattan Developer," *The New York Times*, August 26: Section B, pp. 1, 4.

19. Applebaum (1976), p. 6.

20. AIA Committee on Design (1974), p. 9.

21. Clifford Weaver and Richard F. Babcock (1979). *City Zoning* (Chicago: Planners Press), pp. 167–180.

22. Michael J. Pittas (1980). "Defining Urban Design," *Urban Design International*, 1: 40.

23. Thomas Nally (1977). "Design Review Alternative Models of Administration in Boston," M. Arch/M.C.P. thesis, MIT, pp. 191–192.

24. Robert C. Powell (1977). "Governors Square: A Developer Creates an Urban Garden," *Environmental Comment*, March, p. 13.

25. Nally (1977), p. 192.

26. *Ibid.*, pp. 192–193.

27. William Porter (1980). "Urban Design: A Gentle Critique," *Urban Design International*, 1: 54.

28. Robert S. Cook, Jr. (1980). *Zoning for Downtown Urban Design* (Lexington, Mass.: Lexington Books), p. 157.

29. *Ibid.*, pp. 157–158.

30. Jerome L. Hillis and Robert E. Friedman (1975). "The Developmental Impact of Environmental Regulation," *Environmental Comment*, October, p. 5.

31. Donald Canty (1975). "Learning from Atlanta," *AIA Journal*, 63: 33.

32. Beth Dunlop (1975). "An Accidental City with a Laissez-Faire Approach to Planning," *AIA Journal*, 63: 53.

33. *Ibid.*, 54.

34. Brookline, Massachusetts Department of Planning (1977). "Guide to Environmental Design Review": Vol. 1, "For New Construction;" Vol. 2, "For Commercial Facade."

35. During this study the author found extensive literature in regard to these two cities which greatly helped in the research.

36. Robert S. Clark (1976). "Citywide Design Commission Has Been Operating 7 Year Project, Lessons Are Many," *Practicing Planner*, 6: 37.

37. Rai Okamoto and Frank E. Williams (1969). *Urban Design Manhattan* (New York: The Viking Press), pp. 115, 118.

38. Joseph E. Vitt (1976). "Developing in a Cooperative Environment," *Urban Land*, 37: 3–6.

14
Recommendations

When I could choose from among more than 200 ordinances from towns and cities that already have design review processes in place and when many experts have drawn up model ordinances, why do I presume to make recommendations about the format of a design review process? I do not believe that any of the existing models can be transferred to another city as is or *in toto*. This study has indicated that in each of the four cases examined there are lessons to be learned, lessons which are generally applicable to other cities. Likewise, I have made a special effort to learn which aspects of the cases were especially successful or troublesome. It is my intention to present recommendations in a practical way, allowing the reader to begin more easily the development of his/her own design review process, one that may be made to fit his/her particular urban development. I shall also lead the reader through the maze of environmental conditions that may be present in his/her city in order to suggest the building of a review process which functions effectively in its unique urban environment.

Ground Rules for Successful Design Review Processes

Certain prerequisites to effective design review must be followed regardless of the kind of environment a city has. These include a well established planning program, a clear statement of purpose based on community goals and needs, a carefully outlined description of procedure which avoids complexities, qualified urban design staff and/or review board, citizen participation, and lobbying to improve the total planning/urban design process.

A Well Established Planning Program

Usually, urban design review is an offshoot of a planning program that is already in place. However, before a city darts off in another and new direction—design review—its planning program should be in good order. The deficiencies in the planning program can have repercussions in the review process (and vice versa, of course). Citizen acceptance, after all, is partly based on seeing that these efforts work and do what they are supposed to do.

Planning programs and design review are not efforts to be undertaken lightly. Once again I warn against importing someone else's planning program or design review without considering its local implications. Mazanec's comments may help to clarify my point:

> State, metropolitan, and local planners have failed to produce urban management plans that are clear, consistent, and capable of being implemented. The consequence of this failure is that the environmental movement has filled the land use planning void with laws, regulations, and agencies addressing each incidence of land use abuse or mismanagement.[1]

A Clear Statement of Purpose

The important thing is *to have a plan*, a basic plan for the community with an arrangement for urban design that fits that community. Raymond says "There is a great deal to be gained from trying to follow an overall plan even if it has to be changed frequently in response to changed objectives brought on by unforeseen circumstances."[2]

Consider Kinsey's study of Atlantic City's "renaissance" which has lessons for other areas planning to allow casinos: "Plan ahead . . . with a clear master plan, a good zoning ordinance, and an adequate development review process."[3] Further suggestions: use a "pre-application conference . . . prepare for fanciful architecture and insist on appropriate designs."[4] Kinsey is saying, in other words, don't transfer Las Vegas to Atlantic City. This is no easy task: time, money, and expertise are required if good results are to be accomplished in the design review process.

There are differences of opinion concerning the proper location for review procedures. Should they be established as part of the zoning procedures (as in FASD), or should they be carried out by a separate agency? There is no easy answer; certainly, the thorough research about your city that you are going to undertake to improve your plan or before establishing a design review process may offer some hints concerning the proper placement in your city. Zoning regulations may be too restrictive and may not allow the flexibility which is essential for design review regulations.

Siegan sees some basic problems with zoning itself because, he charges, "it is largely controlled by the dominant political forces of the community." What, Siegan asks, are local legislators to do "when a certain zoning law says one thing and 20 or 50 screaming constituents insist it should be interpreted differently?" He makes a strong case for "dismantling the [zoning] system and reducing the powers of the local legislators." He cites Houston as a case in point: "It has never adopted zoning. Instead, . . . [Houston has] a *limited* [my emphasis] number of specific land use regulations designed to cope with specific land use problems." Siegan further says that competition has been a force to compel developers to maintain amenities.[5]

Weismantel has proposed a CUD (Code for Urban Design) which he suggests as "a substitute for the zoning and subdivision control enabling acts."[6] San Francisco went this route with its Urban Design Plan. Jacobs states that "the substance of the [urban design] plan is policy—specific policy to judge specific proposals for changing the city . . . a working tool to be incorporated into the city's master plan . . . a continuing guide for the future physical development of San Francisco."[7]

A Procedural Description

I have spoken before of the importance of written procedures and consideration of preparing a design manual. A chain of logical steps must be established in order to specify the administrative procedures, to outline the step-by-step process a developer must follow, as well as to reduce the time a developer has to spend searching for information, and finally to reduce the time required for the process itself.

Keep the regulations simple. There is "folly [in] . . . continuing to pursue design excellence via escalations in the stringency and complexity of design regulation."[8] Here again the prohibition against taking over someone else's urban design procedure can be mentioned in a different light. Weaver and Babcock wisely point out that the written word of land use regulations "does not reveal what is really happening . . . how the zoning process [in this case] really works."[9] Their "Methodology: Observations From the Growing Edge" is well worth reading and applying while you are simplifying your procedures for urban design review. Heed Cook's admonition as well: the urban plan that "appears to be working well at a given moment may be successful only because it is at a particular stage in its evolution."[10]

Qualified Staff/Review Board

There is a definite need for a qualified urban design staff to carry out the review process. But, you say, my city can't afford an urban design "staff." Point well taken, but consider what Weismantel says:

> Boston data also shows that the largest two per cent of building permit applications by estimated cost per permit account were from 50–70% of annual building construction. This suggests that a city might have one highly paid urban designer to review that two per cent of all applications which bulk so large, and hire recent graduates to look after the rest.[11]

Perhaps you'll have to think even smaller and look for a planner with some expertise in urban design.

Recall that in Chapters 1 and 13 we drew a distinction among architects, urban designers, and planners. Regardless of which hat an individual wears when he comes to the reviewing process, he must have applicable technical skills or gain them quickly. Jacobs discusses this problem:

> On the other hand, the architects [on the committee preparing an urban design plan for San Francisco] played roles that were quite different from those they played when they were representing clients at the planning department. Here they did seem to be wearing public as opposed to private hats. They offered and supported proposals to restrict building height, color, shape, and

bulk, as well as the disposition of public property for development purposes.[12]

An urban design review member should have political know-how in both technical and political areas, for in a sense urban designers are truly in the middle; they must serve the public's interests, but they also must understand the developer-architect's problems and allow for creativity and innovation which can also be of public benefit. The urban designer must know when input from other disciplines is needed in design review so that he/she can call on experts in law, transportation, environmental issues, and so forth.

I have already mentioned that the laws applicable to a city may provide for an appointed design review board. I repeat my caution that it may be difficult to get "qualified" persons to serve and that they will need a crash course in urban design if they are to make meaningful decisions. The law will also specify whether these boards are solely advisory in nature or whether they may themselves make urban design review decisions. I also have spoken of the importance of the reviewer's (whether professional or lay) having the ear of the chief executive of the city. Certainly, cities with an appointed board should have skilled professionals to guide that board toward "good" design for that city.

Urban design professionals have a tendency to downgrade lay boards and to assert that professionals can do it better. Perhaps so, but they do not always have the legal opportunity to try. Advisory lay boards can play an importat role in bringing "good design" to their communities. Seattle is a prime example.[13] Professional staff with technical and political know-how can help a lay board gain necessary background and can influence design decisions indirectly. It is not easy to be a staff member in these circumstances. McHarg sees planners as "catalysts" and agents "for outlining available options."[14]

Citizen Participation

Citizen input is important from the very beginning of the review process: to establish the overall goals and objectives of the process, to set urban design policies, plans, and guidelines, and to review specific projects as they occur.

No plan can be relevant or effective without public review and support, and this cannot be emphasized enough. . . . [The plan] must stand firmly as a basis for community agreement and commitment to a better city, a lasting set of reference points for rational decision making.[15]

When Atlanta enacted a CDBG program, the city was divided into planning districts, and citizens helped draft 40 district plans.[16]

Lobbying

Gaining consensus on "good" urban design may not be as difficult as it seems at first, if the urban designers provide meaningful non-controversial information which builds a general frame of reference for "good" design before it is applied to a specific case.[17]

Lobbying has negative connotations to many people and an image of deals being made under the table or in smoke-filled rooms. It is lobbying I am suggesting, nonetheless. Why? Let us suppose you are Mr./Ms. Citizen about to begin your first term on City X's Design Review Board. After a few meetings I feel quite sure you will want to make changes in City X's procedures *and* discard completely regional, state, and federal regulations that "interfere" with implementing good design in City X. As Mazanec says, "Dealing with this proliferation of environmental review is beyond the scope of environmental planners. The problem has become a question of linking the growth and development plans of different levels of government to streamline the development review process."[18]

Jurisdictional problems also beset the design review process: whose prerogative is it to review a project which is clearly within City X but has regional implications? Does Project B *really* require that an EIA (Environmental Impact Assessment) be completed to fulfill federal obligations?

Consider the situation in the Potomac River Basin—"complex and an excellent example of the difficulties inherent in the decision-making process for planning in the nation's capital and its surroundings." Involved are four states; the EPA; the U.S. Corps of Engineers; the Federal Power Commission; and the Departments of Interior, Defense, Agriculture, and HHS. An Interstate Commission of the Potomac Basin was formed in 1940 and given an advisory role. Small wonder that "it remains entangled in a maze of agencies characteristic of decision-making Washington style."[19]

Sometimes, amazingly enough, the impetus for regional cooperation can come from business. Lancaster, Pennsylvania, is an example. In 1975 Armstrong Cork Company and National Central Bank convened a small group of leading business executives to "examine community conditions and determine whether effective business leadership would improve the quality of community life." They looked at all phases of "crucial" regional issues.[20]

The result has been most salubrious: a downtown recovery plan fostered by cooperation between business and government; The Greater Lancaster Corporation which besides downtown efforts has a goal to invent and operate a continuing region-wide community development process; Lancaster Tomorrow, a joint venture among The Greater Lancaster Corporation, the city, and the county; and Lancaster Today, an inventory of present-day community life, agreement on issues, and publication as a basis for planning the future of the Lancaster area. These procedures are described as a "choice-making strategy: management capability, community climate, understanding, and a strategic agenda" showing the importance of communication because "nearly everyone" in a community is a "choice-maker."[21]

Mazanec chronicles how the Metropolitan Council in Minneapolis-St. Paul has been an effective lobbying agent at the state level above and the municipal level below its own range of responsibility.[22] If you need convincing on the pervasive federal role in environmental matters, see Sharp, "The Increasing Federal Role in Land Use Control"—and then try to enumerate federal legislation that has come since his article was published in 1978.[23] In several places I have suggested simplification of procedures for urban design review. Lobbying to remove extraneous, contradictory, and duplicative regulations will help bring about a simplification.

These, then, are the ground rules for a successful design review process. The city seeking to improve an existing process must examine its model carefully to be sure these conditions are met and amend its model as needed. A city which wishes to establish a design review process must build in and on these prerequisites.

I shall present two sets of recommendations in as much detail as possible. The first deals with making particular aspects of design review models more effective, and the second focuses on understanding interactions of a model with environmental conditions. My recommendations will assist all cities, both those wishing to improve an existing review process and those seeking to adopt an urban design review process.

Improving Existing Models

In which aspects of a design review model are we able to affect change regardless of the environment where that model is applied? The framework of the recommendations for change is based on the comparative study and classification of the four urban design review models in Chapter 7. I therefore recommend determining the range of a model according to its four components: approach, nature, elements, and management.

Approach

The most practical range for the approach to an urban design review model is between semi-self-administering and semidiscretionary. It is clear that while the completely self-administering approach is predictable and easier to apply and enforce, it is too rigid and therefore is not practical for that reason. It definitely does not allow for innovation and creativity and could result in uninteresting environments not really reflective of the public's interests. Likewise, it is very difficult to establish an approach that is truly self-administering, as, for example, in New York City's FASD. The completely discretionary approach, on the other hand, is likely to be counterproductive.

A formal approach which is clearly spelled out in a city's zoning ordinance is definitely the most practical because it allows a developer's team to know in advance what is expected from them and what kind of process they must follow. This also makes for a good working relationship between reviewer and developer throughout the design review process—their roles are clearly defined. Minneapolis's formal approach shows the advantages of such a system.

The focus of the approach for a city's urban design review

should be both project- and process-oriented. While it is highly desirable for a city to work diligently toward and finally to establish both approaches, either approach may be practical if a city wishes to concentrate on one rather than the other. Here is a point at which the particular characteristics of the city may be of importance, however. Recall that San Francisco has chosen to use both project as well as process approaches; Boston and Minneapolis have established project approaches, while New York City has a process approach.

Nature

The geographic scope of the urban design review should be city-wide, but the process should include provisions for special districts. It is evident that most cities have special areas that are of a specific character with a sensitivity to economic forces or other factors which make them unique. Even in San Francisco's city-wide urban design plan, for example, there are various special districts. Presently, many cities are placing considerable emphasis on detailed study of such districts. Special districts also may bridge the gap between traditional zoning regulations and various control measures aimed at preserving particular types of areas, such as historic or natural preservation districts. The distinction is that the character of each such district is unique and not liable to broad categorization in a city-wide urban design plan.[24]

In addition, designation of special districts allows special regulations to be used exclusively in that district, but compatibility with the city-wide urban design plan is assured. In fact, the only way the public interest in a special district may be guaranteed is through a city-wide plan allowing for special districts. It is desirable to "protect natural or man-made features which are important to the community and are threatened by pressures for new development."[25]

Control of all types of development produces better environmental results than specifying controls for only one specific type of development. However, there are various controls for different types of development. Minneapolis's control of residential development exclusively with the Concept Plan Review was less advantageous than the other three models' broader controls for all types of development.

Incorporating the majority of urban design review guidelines into a city's zoning ordinance builds in more support and strength for the urban designers and other review members. However, limited discretionary power should be excluded from the zoning ordinance and specified in the urban design review process itself. Guidelines which are too rigid are not practical; but, by the same token, too general a set of guidelines and standards is also impractical and may leave too much discretion in the hands of the reviewers. Recall, for instance, what happened in the Charleston Savings Bank review process when Sloan exercised his discretion in reviewing the project.

Yet, every detail and interpretation of the guidelines cannot be placed into a city's zoning ordinance. An overall urban design plan or set of urban design criteria should be specified and included in a manual to guide developers through the process. The importance of such a manual or plan has been shown in the discussion of San Francisco's successful urban design review process and in the contrasting lack of details in the BRA design review process.

Prescriptive guidelines are necessary components of an urban design review. It is desirable that these guidelines be established in conjunction with suggested prototypes and with references to other successful projects. Details of the guidelines—possibly including illustrations—may also be part of a design manual. Each type of guidelines has certain advantages. In combination, the three aspects of guidelines form a more productive and advantageous urban design review process: amount of detail included in the guidelines, the degree of discretion allowed the architect, and the types of examples of satisfactory performance.

Performance guidelines are also highly desirable. Performance guidelines are "general criteria for assessing the appropriateness of a particular development for a specific area. . . . They are concerned with establishing minimum requirements to ensure an acceptable level of performance or compatibility."[26] Of prime importance are provisions to ensure that developers follow through on plans they have presented. Penalties for nonperformance must be considered, and monitoring mechanisms to continue supervision to occupancy of a project may be required.

Incentives are advantageous to a developer according to the nature of the trade-off and to the public as long as it receives something equal in exchange. Incentives may be more productive than controls in persuading a developer to take the larger public interests into consideration.

> Whereas controls attempt to coerce the right result, incentives seek to create the right result by providing a variety of benefits to the developer. They tend to fall into general categories: trade-offs or bonuses, and financial aids.[27]

Incentive zoning can be more successful in guarding the public's interests than restrictive legislation.

Elements

The elements of an urban design review model should include guidelines to assure compatibility with the surrounding environment, a "positive environmental, social, and economic impact on adjoining uses." A second element essential to an urban design review model is conservation: "the use of nonrenewable resources to achieve a workable, comfortable environment."[28] In their recommendations for environmental planning in San Diego, Lynch and Appleyard called this element "natural resource analysis"[29] and place it between urban design and growth studies. The final basic element of an urban design review model to be addressed in the guidelines is "appropriate physical forms and types of uses"—architectural issues.[30]

Management

The urban design body that manages the urban design review should be tied closely under the chief executive of the city, and the lines of communication must be open. Whether the urban design review body is a part of the department of planning, a development authority, or another public agency is not of great consequence, as long as communication with the top management of the city is possible, likely through specific provision for this in the design review process. Finally, eight to twelve weeks is a reasonable time span for the completion of an urban design review and gives the developer's team as well as city officials sufficient time to handle the project review. See Figure 14-1 for a summary of recommended improvements to existing models.

Interaction of Models with Environments

Many environmental factors may influence the selection of an urban design review model that is appropriate for a particular environment, and a city should not attempt to establish an urban design review process without first assessing the unique social, economic, and political characteristics that are currently present in its environment, those which will influence the success of the design review process chosen. These factors do not influence all aspects of the model, however; some may affect all the components—approach, nature, and elements—while others only affect a few. In Chapter 13, we enumerated and discussed numerous environmental factors identified in the four case studies and in other research. A summary list may be found at the end of the chapter. The reader/user may find it useful to consider the

Approach
Semi-self-administering to semidiscretionary
Formal most practical
Combination of project- and process-orientation

Nature
City-wide application with consideration of possible use of special districts
Covering all types of development
Guidelines placed in city zoning ordinances, urban design plans, and/or
    urban design manuals
Prescriptive and performance guidelines included
Incentives or bonuses for inclusion of amenities

Elements
Compatibility
External impacts
Architectural issues

Management
Directly under chief executive of the city
8-12 weeks—reasonable length for review process

Figure 14-1: Outline of recommendations for improvement of design review process in any environment.

likelihood of other environmental factors in a particular city, factors unique to his/her city and to draw up his/her own list. The next task is to show the interaction of these factors with the components they affect, to decide the importance of each in your city.

The format of this interaction follows logically from consideration of the three major components of a model: approach, nature, and elements. It easily lends itself to the compiling of the useful, informative and self-explanatory lists that follow. After stating a choice of component, I show all major factors influencing the selection of such a choice. Some environmental factors appear in almost all the lists, indicating that they may be influential on all aspects of the model; others only appear in a few places, influencing only a few aspects.

These lists will suggest to the reader/user a basic framework for testing an existing process or for establishing a new urban design review model because they focus on the appropriateness of the various model components in particular environmental situations. There is no claim that these lists cover all possibilities. Again the reader/user must consider his/her particular environment. Differing community values or very specific environmental factors peculiar to a city may change the influence of other factors in the interactions listed. Knowledge of the particular economic, social, and political climates of a city is critical to the success of urban design review and to serving the public's interests.

Approach

Self-administering.—A self-administering approach implies the use of detailed guidelines to explain criteria the reviewing body will use to judge the proposed project's design. Most often, the concern is functional elements of design. The developer knows in advance the guidelines for review (particularly if there is a design manual). He can anticipate exactly what is to be expected of him. The result of the review in this case may not be better design but better functional elements. Approach may be self-administering when there is:

- low political support
- limited resource availability
- moderate/low level of concern by public officials

- moderate/low level of citizen support and involvement
- slow-growing market pressure
- very sensitive and vulnerable urban setting
- concern only for functional elements
- small staff of qualified urban designers
- large city bureaucracy
- predictable circumstances
- desire or need to:
  —eliminate/minimize necessity for design review process
  —minimize time factor.

Semi-self-administering.—A semi-self-administering approach is a compromise between the self-administering and the discretionary approaches, maintaining more features of the former than the latter. This approach implies a higher commitment to urban design review. The developer has a little more latitude for discretion than in the self-administering approach.

Approach may be semi-self-administering when there is:

- moderate political support
- moderate resource availability
- moderate/high level of concern by public officials
- moderate citizen support and involvement
- moderate market pressure
- moderately sized design review staff
- high level of design review process
- concern for functional and aesthetic design elements
- large city bureaucracy
- desire or need to:
  —minimize subjective personal influence
  —minimize time factor
  —eliminate outside route of influence
  —make outcome predictable.

Semidiscretionary.—A semidiscretionary approach is a second compromise between the self-administering and the discretionary approaches with more aspects of the latter than the former. Note that the developer now has some options, and the design review staff has an opportunity for limited discretion.

Approach may be semidiscretionary when there is:

- moderate political support

- moderate/high resource availability
- high level of concern by public officials
- moderate level of citizen support and involvement
- moderate market pressure
- larger staff of qualified urban designers
- concern for functional and aesthetic elements
- high level of cooperation between public and private sectors
- smaller city bureaucracy
- high level of cooperation among city agencies
- desire or need to:
    —allow negotiation between city and developer
    —allow more freedom for creativity and innovation
    —allow options to developer.

Discretionary.—With the discretionary approach, the reviewers generally have centralized power and authority. A project-oriented approach is typical. The developer is at the mercy of the reviewers with few trade-offs he can use to advantage. It is more difficult for him to avoid design review.

Approach may be discretionary when there is:

- high political support
- high resource availability
- high level of concern by public officials
- high level of citizen support and involvement
- moderate/low market pressure
- concern for aesthetic vs. functional elements
- presence of qualified urban designers
- small city bureaucracy
- high level of cooperation between public and private sectors
- high level of planning activity plus urban design process
- high level of cooperation among city agencies
- low potential for outside influences
- desire or need to:
    —limit the freedom for creativity and innovation
    —limit options to developer
    —limit extent of negotiation between city and developer.

Nature

The nature of the design review process refers to the degree or level of detail in the guidelines. I also include in this category whether the guidelines are defined by performance or prescriptive standards and whether these standards are described through prototypes or with references to specific design. A factor to consider with regard to the nature of design review is the extent of control that is desired. Performance standards state a criterion or a quantifiable standard that the developer and his architect must meet. No test is required in prescriptive standards, but they specify characteristics of the final design. At times, a combination of performance and prescriptive standards best suits the needs of a city.

City-wide application.—Application of urban design review may be city-wide when there is:

- moderate/high political support
- high resource availability
- moderate/high level of concern by public officials
- moderate/high level of citizen support and involvement
- lack/minimum of districts/neighborhoods with special character and/or value
- homogeneous urban pattern
- need or desire to:
    —establish overall framework of urban design guidelines.

Special district application.—Application of urban design review may be only in special districts when there is:

- low/moderate political support
- moderate resource availability
- moderate/high level of concern by public officials
- moderate level of citizen support and involvement
- high market pressure in a specific area
- concern only for aesthetic *or* functional elements
- heterogeneous urban pattern
- number of different neighborhoods/districts with special character
- need or desire to:
    —establish specific guidelines for a specific area
    —use incentive/bonus system.

City-wide and special district application.—Application of urban design review may be both city-wide and in special districts when there is:

- moderate political support
- high resource availability
- high level of concern by public officials
- high level of citizen support and involvement
- mix of heterogeneous and homogeneous areas in the urban pattern
- concern for both aesthetic and functional elements
- high level of planning activities
- high availability of qualified urban designers
- clear and thorough understanding of urban design goals and objectives by public and public officials.

Guidelines.—Guidelines may be placed into city zoning ordinances when there is:

- moderate/low political support
- moderate resource availability
- moderate level of concern by public officials
- moderate level of citizen support and involvement
- high market pressure
- system of incentives/bonuses
- low level of cooperation between public and private sectors
- low/moderate level of overall planning activities
- low level of cooperation among various city agencies
- desire or need to minimize:
    —number of review sessions
    —time required for review process
    —debate and controversy
- desire or need to:
    —eliminate outside route of influence
    —spell out purpose and intent of guidelines clearly in the law.

Design manual/guidebook.—Design manual/guidebook may be developed where there is:

- moderate/high level of political support
- moderate/high resource availability
- high level of concern by public officials

- concern for both aesthetic and functional elements
- moderate level of cooperation between public and private sectors
- moderate level of planning activity
- moderate level of cooperation among various city agencies
- moderate sized city bureaucracy
- desire or need to:
    —explain the guidelines in a more understandable way
    —reduce time spent on design review process.

Urban design plan.—Urban design plan may be developed when there is:

- moderate political support
- high resource availability
- high level of concern by public officials
- high level of citizen support and involvement
- moderate/high market pressure
- concern for both aesthetic and functional elements
- moderate sized city bureaucracy
- high level of cooperation between public and private sectors
- high overall level of planning activities
- well organized department of planning and/or urban design
- highly qualified urban design staff available
- high level of cooperation among various city agencies
- desire or need to:
    —explain/define urban design goals and objectives
    —preserve overall urban fabric adequately
    —eliminate overlapping work of city agencies
    —explain guidelines adequately
- well organized department of planning and/or urban design
- high level of cooperation among various city agencies
- medium/small sized city bureaucracy
- desire or need to:
    —make options available to developers
    —allow for creativity and innovation.

Elements

The elements of design control describe those aspects of a proposed design that the city wishes to control through design review. These elements may include everything from the compatability of a building to its surroundings to architectural details. The concerns of a city—or at least of the persons who established the urban design process—are revealed by the elements that are to be reviewed. What are the concerns? How broad is the scope of issues to be covered by review? An extensive list of elements to be reviewed may indicate either a sophisticated use of design review or inclusion of a proliferation of details that could become unenforceable.

Compatability.—Elements of urban design would include only those concerned with compatability when there is:

- low political support
- low resource availability
- moderate/low level of concern by public officials
- low market pressure
- low availability of urban design staff
- low overall level of planning activity.

Prescriptive guidelines.—Prescriptive guidelines may be developed when there is:

- moderate/low political support
- moderate/low resource availability
- moderate/low level of concern by public officials
- moderate/low level of citizen support and involvement
- moderate/high market pressure
- moderate/low overall level of planning activities
- large city bureaucracy
- desire or need to minimize:
    —options for developers
    —outside routes of influence
- desire or need to:
    —reduce level of creativity and innovation
    —control vulnerable area(s) of the city.

Prescriptive and performance guidelines.—A combination of prescriptive and performance guidelines may be developed when there is:

- moderate/high level of political support
- high resource availability
- high level of citizen support and involvement

- high market pressure
- qualified urban design staff available
- clearly defined urban design function/scope
- concern for balance of aesthetic and functional elements
- high overall level of planning activity
- moderate/high level of cooperation between public and private sectors.

Compatability and external impact.—Elements of urban design would include those concerned with compatability *and* external impact when there is:

- moderate political support
- moderate resource availability
- moderate/low level of concern by public officials
- moderate/high level of citizen support and involvement
- moderate/high market pressure
- high availability of qualified urban design staff
- concern for both aesthetic and functional elements
- moderate/high level of overall planning activity
- well organized department of planning and/or urban design
- moderate/high level of cooperation between public and private sectors.

Compatability, external impact, and architectural issues.—Elements of urban design would include compatability, external impact *and* architectural issues when there is:

- moderate/high political support
- high resources availability
- high level of concern by public officials
- high level of citizen support and involvement
- adequate number of qualified urban designers
- clear definition of scope and elements of the urban design function
- high level of planning activity
- well organized department of planning and/or urban design
- small/medium sized city bureaucracy
- desire or need to limit:
    —availability of options to developers
    —level of freedom for creativity and innovation by architects
    —time of urban design review process

• desire or need to:
  —eliminate outside routes of influence.

Notes

1. Robert C. Mazanec (1977). "Let's Put the Plan Back into. . . . . ning," *Urban Land*, Vol 36(5):77.

2. George M. Raymond (1978). "The Role of the Physical Urban Planner," in Robert W. Burchell and George Sternlieb, eds. *Planning Theory in the 1980's* (New Brunswick, N.J.: Center for Urban Policy Research), p. 4.

3. David N. Kinsey (1979). "A Partnership for Casino Development: State Environmental Perspectives on Atlantic City's Renaissance," *Environmental Comment*, August, p. 11.

4. *Ibid.*, pp. 11, 13.

5. Bernard H. Siegan (1977). "Zoning Incentives: Do They Give Us What We Really Want?" *Environmental Comment*, January, pp. 4–5.

6. William Weismantel (1970). "Legislating the Urban Design Process," *Urban Law Annual* (St. Louis, Mo., Washington University Law School), p. 196.

7. Allan B. Jacobs (1971). "San Franciscans Seek to Save Their City," *AIA Journal*, 56:32.

8. Clifford L. Weaver and Richard F. Babcock (1979). *City Zoning* (Chicago: American Planning Association), p. 301.

9. *Ibid.*, p. 23.

10. Robert S. Cook, Jr. (1980). *Zoning for Downtown Design* (Lexington, Mass: Lexington Books), p. 152.

11. Weismantel (1970), 125.

12. Allan B. Jacobs (1978). *Making City Planning Work* (Chicago: American Society of Planning Officials), p. 198.

13. Robert S. Clark (1976). "Citywide Design Commission Has Been Operating 7 Year Project, Lessons Are Many," *Practicing Planner*, 6:31–39.

14. Ian McHarg (1980). "Ecological Planning: The Planner as Catalyst," in Robert W. Burchell and George Sternlieb, eds., *Planning Theory in the 1980's* (New Brunswick, N.J.: Center for Urban Policy Research), p. 13.

15. Jacobs (1971), 32.

16. Beth Dunlop (1975). "An Accidental City with a Laissez-Faire Approach to Planning," *AIA Journal*, 63:55.

17. See, for example, Bruce Hendler (1977). *Caring For the Land* (Chicago:

American Society of Planning Officials), 93 pp. This is a well illustrated volume with an annotated bibliography of technical assistance.

18. Mazanec (1977), 77.

19. Colden Florance (1974). "Frustrated Effort to Make Potomac a Model River," *AIA Journal*, 61:56–57.

20. Owen Kugel (1978). "Lancaster, Pennsylvania: A Community That Works," *Urban Land*, 37:4.

21. *Ibid.*, 8.

22. Mazanec (1977), 12–19.

23. James A. Sharp (1978). "The Increasing Federal Role in Land Use Control," *Architectural Record*, 163: 71, 73.

24. Frederick H. Bair, Jr. (1973). "Special Public Interest Districts," in *Planning Advisory Service*, No. 287 (Chicago: American Society of Planning Officials).

25. John L. Kriken (1979). "Urban Design," in Frank S. So *et al.*, eds., *The Practice of Local Government Planning* (Washington: International City Management Association), p. 376.

26. *Ibid.*, p. 377.

27. *Ibid.*, p. 378.

28. *Ibid.*, p. 355.

29. Kevin Lynch and Donald Appleyard (1976). *Progress in Paradise?* Vol. 2 (San Diego, Cal.: City of San Diego Urban Design Task Force), p. 14.

30. Kriken, p. 355.

Epilogue

Urban design and planning efforts are frustrating to those who are committed to improving the environment in which we live. Sometimes it all seems hardly worthwhile! Take heart with these words from Madden:

> Large-scale and fundamental technology like ours interacts with the environment to produce unexpected and unwanted results, but these results could be foreseen if we perceived events in broader perspective. . . . Man through the ages has had to control his culture to survive. A livable environment is a survival issue on Spaceship Earth . . . an issue of inventing a new culture. . . . The benefit of survival and advance would far outweigh the cost in change and adjustment.[1]

Note

1. Carl H. Madden (1971). "The Cost of a Livable Environment," *AIA Journal*, 55: 27, 28, 30.

References

Definition

Appleyard, D. 1977. Guide to planning practice—needs analyses aid priority setting. *Practicing Planner* 7(4): 31-34.

Appleyard, D. & Lynch, K. 1974. *Temporary paradise? A look at the special landscape of the San Diego region.* San Diego, CA: San Diego Department of Planning.

Babcock, R.F. 1966. *The zoning game: Municipal practices & policies.* Madison: University of Wisconsin Press.

Bacon, E.N. 1963. Urban design as a force in comprehensive planning. *Journal of the American Institute of Planners* 29(2): 2-8.

———. 1971. 7 principles for an urban land policy. *Urban Land* 30(4): 3-8.

Bair, F.H., Jr. 1973. *Special public interest district: A multipurpose zoning device.* Planning advisory service report no. 287. Chicago: American Society of Planning Officials.

Barett, D.R. 1973. *Inventive zoning for Boston.* Boston, MA: Boston Redevelopment Authority.

Barnett, J. 1970. Urban design as part of the governmental process. *Architectural Record* 147(1): 131-150.

———. 1974. *Urban design as a public policy.* New York: Architectural Record Books.

———. 1978. On urban design. *Urban Design* 9(2): 18-23.

Blumenfield, H. 1967. The role of design. *Journal of the American Institute of Planners* 33(5): 304-323.

Bosselman, F. & Siemon, C. 1976. Improving due process in local zoning decisions. *Environmental Comment* August: 14-16.

Chamber of Commerce of the United States. 1969. *Form, design & a more attractive city environment.* Washington, DC.

Cooke, T. 1976. Guide to planning practice—a process for community design. *Practicing Planner* 6(1): 27-30.

Cooper, A. 1973. Zoning with the user in mind. *AIA Journal* 60(6): 42-46.

Cramer, R.D. 1960. Zoning and what we can do to improve it. *AIA Journal* 33(1): 90-94.

Creighton, T.H. 1977. Urban design, frustrating fate. *AIA Journal:* 66(7): 51-53.

Eckbo, G. 1963. Urban design, a definition. *AIA Journal* 40(3): 37-38.

Elliot, D. 1968. The role of design in the governmental process. *Architectural Record* 143(1): 141-144.

Embry, R.C. 1978. Urban environmental design through joint development. *HUD Challenge* 9(9): 8-10.

Euston, A.F., Jr. 1978. The emergence of urban environmental design. *HUD Challenge* 9(9): 2.

_____. 1978. UED in local government. *HUD Challenge* 9(9): 20-21.

Feiss, C. 1973. Planning absorbs zoning. *Journal of the American Institute of Planners* 39(5): 121-126.

Gulak, M.B. 1978. Urban design goals as public policy issues: An evaluation. In *Proceedings, First National Conference on Urban Design*, Ferebee, A., ed. Washington, DC: RC Publications.

Hoppenfeld, M. 1960. The role of planning in city design—with reference to center-city Philadelphia. *Journal of the American Institute of Planners* 26(5): 98-103.

_____. 1961. The role of design in city planning. *AIA Journal* 35(5): 40-44.

_____. 1963. The practice of urban design: Some contemporary examples. *Journal of the American Institute of Planners* 29(7): 95-110.

Jacobs, A.B. 1978. *Making city planning work*. Chicago: American Society of Planning Officials.

_____. 1980. A planner's view of the city. *Planning* 46(3): 20-23. .

_____. 1980. Planners, plan thy own cities. *American Planning Association News* June: 5.

Kent, T.J., Jr. 1964. *The urban general plan*. San Francisco, CA: Chandler.

Kriken, J.L. 1979. Urban design. In *The practice of local government planning*, So, F.S. et al., eds. Washington, DC: International City Management Association.

Kriken, J.L. & Torrey, I.P. 1973. *Developing urban design mechanisms.* Planning advisory service report no. 296. Chicago: American Society of Planning Officials.

Lefcoe, G. 1975. How taxes affect urban design—& how to make them do a better job of it. *Real Estate Law Journal* 4: 244-262.

Leslie, R.B. 1975. Planning & aesthetic zoning—getting more out of what we've got. *Journal of Urban Law* 52: 1033-1062.

Lu, W. 1976. *The role of urban design in local government.* Dallas: Dallas Department of Urban Planning.

———. 1978. Urban design research, a structure. *Urban Design* 9(2): 42-45.

Lynch, K. & Appleyard, D. 1976. *Progress in paradise?* San Diego, CA: City of San Diego Urban Design Task Force, Vol. I and II.

Mansotti, L.H. & Selfon, B.I. 1969. Aesthetic zoning & the policy power. *Journal of Urban Law* 46(4): 773-788.

Marcus, M. & West, J. 1972. Urban design through zoning: The Special Greenwich Street Development District. *Planner's Notebook* 2(5): 2-8.

Mayer, A. 1971. Notes toward a definition of urban design. *Architectural Forum* 135(4): 60-63.

Meshenberg, M.J. 1976. *The administration of flexible zoning techniques.* Planning advisory service report no. 318. Chicago: American Society of Planning Officials.

Montgomery, R. 1965. Improving the design process in urban renewal. *Journal of the American Institute of Planners* 31(2): 7-20.

Parker, I.J. 1977. Comprehensive design zones: Using zoning to protect the environment. *Environmental Comment* January: 20-23.

Pittas, M.J. 1980. Defining urban design. *Urban Design International* 1(2): 40.

Porter, W.L. 1980. Urban design: A gentle critique. *Urban Design International* 1(2): 47, 54, 56.

Reichek, J. 1962. Questions concerning urban design principles. *AIA Journal* 38(6): 102-103.

Robbins, J. 1974. The public practice of urban design in a California community. *AIA Journal* 62(5): 24-27.

San Diego Urban Design Task Force. 1976. *Progress in paradise?* Volume I-II.

Schlivek, L.B. 1975. Urban design & planning are paying dividends, examples. *AIA Journal* 64(2): 17.

Schwarz, E. 1976. Superb incentive zoning program. *Design & Environment* 7(2): 28-33.

Sharp, J.A. 1978. Increasing federal role in land use control. *Architectural Record* 163(4): 71, 73.

Siegan, B.H. 1977. Zoning incentives: Do they give us what we really want? *Environmental Comment* January: 4-5.

Slayton, W.L. 1968. Who is the urban design client? *AIA Journal* 49(2): 59-61.

Spreiregen, P.D. 1964. Government & urban design. *AIA Journal* 42(3): 65-80.

——. 1965. Comprehensive role for urban design. *AIA Journal* 43(4): 16-21.

——. 1965. Urban design contract. *AIA Journal* 44(3): 44-49.

——. 1966. Urban design. *AIA Journal* 45(1): 43-46.

Tomson, B. & Coplan, N. 1970. Aesthetic zoning rationale, part 1. *Progressive Architecture* 51(11): 116.

——. 1970. Aesthetic zoning rationale, part 2. *Progressive Architecture* 51(12): 84.

Trancik, R. & Goodey, B. 1978. Defining urban design. *Urban Design* 9(2): 24-27.

Urban Design Committee. 1964. Government & urban design. *AIA Journal* 42(3): 65-80.

——. 1964. A comprehensive role for urban design. *AIA Journal* 42(5): 73-96.

Urban design in practice. 1965. *AIA Journal* 44(5): 43-47.

U.S. Environmental Protection Agency, Office of Research & Development. 1974. *Environmental management & local government.* Washington, DC.

Vitt, J.E. 1978. Developing in a cooperative environment. *Urban Land* 37(10): 3-6.

Weese, H. 1961. Architectural controls, its effect on cities. *AIA Journal* 35(3): 56-58.

Weismantel, W. 1970. Legislating the urban design process. *Urban Law Annual*. Saint Louis, MO: Washington University Law School, pp. 196-230.

Wittenberg, G.G. 1965. Politics of urban design. *AIA Journal* 44(4): 75-79.

Wolfe, M.R. & Shinn, R.D. 1970. Urban design within the comprehensive planning process. Seattle: University of Washington.

Practice

Abercrombie, S. 1978. Winning the third battle of Trenton. *Urban Design* 9: 26-31.

Adams, G.D. 1980. San Francisco: Utopia reconsidered. *Planning* 46(3): 20-23.

American Institute of Architects Regional/Urban Design Assistance Team for Fairfax County (VA) Division of Planning. 1972. *Fairfax County.*

Analysis of urban design issue of Harvard Square. 1975. *Progressive Architecture* 56(1): 70.

Appelbaum, R.P. 1976. Natural for whom? Studying growth in Santa Barbara. *Environmental Comment* February: 3-7.

Arlington (MA) Department of Planning & Community Development. 1977. *Sign sense.*

Bacon, E.N. 1961. Downtown Philadelphia developments. *Architectural Record* 129(5): 131-146.

Baltimore Department of Housing & Community Development. 1970. *Oldtown development guide.*

Barefoot, N., Jr. 1961. Redesigning Philadelphia. *AIA Journal* 35(6): 91-95.

Barett, D.R. 1973. *Incentive zoning for Boston.* Boston, MA: Boston Redevelopment Authority.

Barnes, W.A. & Abraham, R. 1979. Pennsylvania Avenue—Main Street, America comes to life. *Urban Land* 39(6): 12-17.

Beacon Hill Civic Association. 1975. *Beacon Hill architectural* handbook: Guidelines for preservation & modification. Boston, MA.

Bernard Johnson, Inc. 1972. San Marcos urban design study. Houston.

Bloom, M. 1977. The salvation of Times Square as a challenge to urban design. AIA Journal 66(6): 54-59.

Boston Redevelopment Authority. 1969. Downtown design & development study. Boston, MA.

———. 1976. The Tremont Street special district. Boston, MA.

———. 1976. BRA fact book. Boston, MA.

Boston Zoning Ordinance. 1970.

Brambilla, R. & Longo, G. 1979. Learning from Seattle. New York: Institute for Environmental Action.

Brookline (MA) Planning Department. 1976. The comprehensive plan for Brookline, Mass.

Buffalo (NY) Area Office, U.S. Department of Housing and Urban Development. 1971. Whitney neighborhood rehabilitation program.

Burns, J. 1977. Planning for San Francisco. Urban Design 8(2): 24-25.

California environmental quality act. Chapter 5, Section 21160. 1970.

California parks department releases plans to restore San Diego Old Town. 1977. Los Angeles Times March 23: I-23.

Campbell, R. 1977. Charlestown Bank a welcome example of good urban design. Boston Sunday Globe April 10: H-2.

Cappiello, S. 1978. Hoboken: America's comeback town. HUD Challenge 9(2): 2-5.

Carpenter, E.K. 1974. San Francisco Bay, controls on development. Design & Environment 5(4): 16-17.

Carroll, M. 1979. Seattle's Madrona town square. HUD Challenge 10(10): 22-27.

The case for design quality in today's marketplace—four studies of collaboration between architects & developers that explore the arithmetic of excellence. 1977. Architectural Record 162(16): 81-128.

Chicago Department of Urban Renewal. 1964. Lincoln Park project I, preliminary proposal. Chicago.

City of New York Zoning Ordinance. 1975. Chapter 7, Special Fifth Avenue District, section 87-065, p. 417; & section 87-08 & 87-09, p. 418.

_____. 1975. Chapter 7, Special Greenwich Street development district, sections 86-00 through 86-13.

Clarence S. Stein concerned with designing livable communities. 1976. *Los Angeles Times* December 9: VII-8.

Clarke, J.P.; Katon, P.B. & Travisano, F. 1978. The urban design process in Trenton. *HUD Challenge* 9(9): 12-13.

_____. 1978. Trenton's strategy for neighborhood development. *HUD Challenge* 9(9): 15-16.

Commercial design of chain stores viewed. 1973. *Los Angeles Times* August 13: IV-1.

Cooper, C.C. 1975. *Easter Hill Village: Some social implications of design.* New York: Free Press.

'Critics eye' column on Milwaukee downtown area. 1976. *Milwaukee Journal* June 27: 7-1.

Davis (CA) Planning Department. 1977. Mixed uses: A design and zoning proposal for Davis, California.

Davis, R.E. & Weston, J., eds. 1975. *The special zoning concept in New York City.* New York: New York School for Social Research, Center for New York City Affairs.

Davis, R.P. 1977. Baltimore's implementation mechanisms. *HUD Challenge* 8(1): 17-19.

Design of Lake Village East in Chicago discussed. 1973. *Chicago Tribune* August 19: 6-9.

Detroit City Planning Commission, Design Division. 1970. *Civic Center West.*

_____. 1970. *Inner city design resources.*

_____. 1970. *Orchestra place.*

Downtown Chicago office building boom discussed. 1978. *Chicago Tribune* May 7: VI-1.

Downtown city areas may soon resort to old ideas for shoppers. 1979. *Detroit News* November 23: BW-7.

Eckbo, Dean, Austin & Williams. 1971. *Cypress special: The townscape, urban design, open space element of the general plan, Cypress, California.* Los Angeles: Eckbo, Dean, Austin & Williams.

Euston, A. 1976. Transportation, joint development & environmental design policy. *HUD Challenge* 7(12): 10-12.

Fowler, G. 1980. Planning agency breaks up urban design group. *The New York Times* March 28: A26.

Freeman, A. 1976. AIA urban design team study attempts to help city comeback. *AIA Journal* 65(11): 74-77.

Gapp column on book about urban design focuses on Chicago zoning. 1978. *Chicago Tribune* December 27: 2-4.

Garber, S.R. 1979. The main street project. *HUD Challenge* 10(7): 12-19.

Gearin, P. 1979. Church Street marketplace: Burlington underground. *Environmental Comment* January: 13.

Goldberger, P. 1979. Midtown construction problem of prosperity. *New York Times* July 30: B1 & B4.

Halpern, K. 1978. *Downtown USA: Urban design in nine American cities.* New York: Whitney Library of Design.

Halsey, R.D. 1970. *Parking lot landscaping for shopping centers & industrial uses.* Mountainside, NJ: New Jersey Federation of Planning Officials.

Hardy, Holzman & Pfeiffer. 1976. Saving Grand Central Terminal, urban design study. *Journal of Architectural Education* 30(2): 16-21.

Hass, D.F. 1976. *Evolution & application of design controls on Nantucket Island.* Boston, MA: Society for the Preservation of New England Antiquities.

Hester, R. 1975. Ivory tower designers harm neighborhoods. *Landscape Architecture* 66(3): 296-303.

Hillis, J.L. & Friedman, R.E. 1975. The developmental impact of environmental regulation. *Environmental Comment* October: 1-5.

Humphries, B.K. 1974. Beaumont, Texas: One approach to CBD redevelopment. *Urban Land* 33(8): 16-27.

Inniss, P.L. & Kuwabara, G. 1973. *Model cities urban design: Cheyenne.* Cheyenne, Wyoming: Cheyenne Model Cities Program.

Jacksonville (FL) Area Planning Board. 1971. *Jacksonville form & appearance one.*

Jacobs, A.B. 1971. San Franciscans seek to save their city. *AIA Journal* 56(5): 25-32.

Kansas City Department of City Development. 1978. *Kansas City urban design guidebook: Ways to promote & improve the city's value for investment, living & working*. Kansas City, MO: City Development Department.

Kull, R.B. 1978. Urban environmental quality districts: Cincinnati's example. *Environmental Comment* September: 7-10.

La Puente (CA) Planning Department. 1971. *La Puente environmental design manual*.

Lacey, R.M., Balbach, H.E. & Fittipaldi, J.J. 1978. *Compendium of administrators of land use & related programs*. Springfield, VA: National Technical Information Service.

Lieberman, E. 1977. Baltimore's city hall renovation. *HUD Challenge* 8(1): 19-21.

A look at plazas adjoining high-rises in Chicago. 1973. *Chicago Tribune* July 1: 6-9.

Lopez, C.C. 1979. Dateline: Park Slope, Brooklyn. *HUD Challenge* 10(9): 12-14.

Los Angeles sculptor Isamu Noguchi's "Little Tokyo" plaza design viewed. 1980. *Los Angeles Times* March 31: VI-1.

Louisiana architect comments on urban design at New Orleans meeting. 1972. *New Orleans Times-Picayune* February 6: 6-3.

Lowell (MA) City Development Authority. 1970. *Lowell community renewal program: Urban design study*.

McHarg, I.L. 1969. *Design with nature*. Garden City, NY: Natural History Press.

Malo, P. 1968. *The Binghamton commission on architecture & urban design, the first three years, 1964-1967*. Binghamton, NY: Valley Development Foundation.

Mandelker, D.R. 1976. Mutli-permit procedures in the Hawaiian system of land use control. *Environmental Comment* May: 12-14.

Marcus, N. & Groves, M.W. 1970. *The new zoning: Legal, administrative, & economic concepts & techniques*. New York: Praeger.

Masterson, W. 1975. Coordinated permits: The Washington experience. *Environmental Comment* October: 5-10.

Miller, N. 1977. Dallas—urban design sensitivity. *Urban Design* 8(3): 18-21.

Miner, D.P. 1976. Coordination of development regulation: Untangling the maze. *Environmental Comment* May: 1-10.

Minneapolis Department of Planning & Development. 1968. *Inventory & analysis: Signs on the streets.*

_____. 1969. *Metro center 85.* Eleven reports.

_____. 1969. *Work program: Visual communication study.*

_____. 1973. *Planning & development, Minneapolis skyway system.*

_____. 1976. *City of Minneapolis zoning ordinance.* Concept plan review procedure, section 534.450, (2), (9), p. 3778.

_____. 1977. *An improvement plan for Elliot Park neighborhood.*

_____. 1978. *Minneapolis metro center: Forecasts to 1990.*

_____. 1978. *Minneapolis metro center: Plan to 1990.*

_____. 1978. *Minneapolis metro center: Planning principles.*

_____. 1979. *Loring Park/Loring Heights—policy & design plan.*

_____. 1979. *Minutes of city planning commissioner's meeting.* May 10.

_____. 1979. *Plan for the 1980's: General management implementation.*

_____. 1979. *Plan for the 1980's: Overview.*

_____. 1979. *Plan for the 1980's: Physical environment.*

_____. 1979. *Planning & development, metro center 90.*

_____. 1979. *Zoning & other land use controls.*

Mitchell/McArthur/Gardner/O'Kane Associates 1972. *Pringle Creek urban design study, Salem, Oregon.* Portland, OR: Salem Urban Renewal Agency.

New Bedford (MA). 1975. *Environmental assesement guide for community development; an administrative handbook.*

New York City Department of City Planning. 1975. *New life for plazas.*

_____. 1976. *Plazas for people.*

New York City Planning Commission, Urban Design Group. 1975. *Zoning for housing quality.*

News analysis of how well City of Chicago works. 1977. *Chicago Tribune* February 10: N7-1.

Niagra Frontier Transportation Authority. 1971. *Summary report— Niagra frontier mass transit study.*

O'Mara, W.P. 1978. Regulation: Where do we go from here? *Urban Land* 37(5): 9-15.

Office of Lower Manhattan Development. 1971. Special Greenwich Street Development District. New York City.

———. 1976. *Water Street access & development.* New York City.

Offices of Midtown Planning & Development. (n.d.). Fifth Avenue special zoning district. New York City.

———. (n.d.). The impact of the Fifth Avenue Special District legislation on retail floor space on Fifth Avenue. New York City.

Osman, M.E. 1970. New lessons for urban designers in Old San Juan, Puerto Rico. *AIA Journal* 54(2): 34-36.

Palm Springs (CA). 1970. *Zoning ordinance.*

Patterson, W.T. 1976. *Legal & organization tools & techniques for implementing land use plans: Final report.* West Lafayette, IN: School of Civil Engineering, Purdue University.

Paul Friedburg & Associate/Barton-Aschman Associates. 1973. *Loring Park development urban design plan.* Minneapolis: Paul Friedburg & Associate.

Philadelphia City Planning Commission. 1976. *Philadelphia center city walking tour.*

———. 1979. *Capital program—City of Philadelphia & school district of Philadelphia.*

Planned unit development: A promise with problems. 1973. *Design & Environment* 4(4): 15-19.

Podolske, R.D. & Heglund, C.T. 1976. Skyways in Minneapolis/St. Paul. *Urban Land* 35(8): 3-12.

Raphel, M. 1979. The Gordon's Alley story. *HUD Challenge* 10(4): 22-25.

River plaza described. 1978. *Chicago Tribune* April 2: 6-2.

Roots. 1973. Minneapolis: Heritage Preservation Commission.

Ryan, R.J. 1979. Boston rediscovered. *HUD Challenge* 10(9): 16-23.

San Diego (CA) Department of Planning. 1979. *Progress guide & general plan.*

San Francisco Department of City Planning. (n.d.). *Central waterfront plan: A part of the comprehensive plan of the city & county of San Francisco.*

_____. (n.d.). *Master plan urban design politics & principles relating to the downtown special review area.*

_____. (n.d.). *Urban design guidelines revision.* Draft under preparation by Richard Hedman, urban designer.

_____. 1970. *Citywide urban design plans.* Springfield, VA: National Technical Information Service.

_____. 1970. *Preliminary report No. 4: Existing form & image.* Springfield, VA: National Technical Information Service.

_____. 1970. *Preliminary report No. 5: Urban design principles for San Francisco.*

_____. 1970. *Preliminary report No. 7: Implementation approach.*

_____. 1970. *Preliminary report No. 8: Urban design plans.*

_____. 1971. Resolution No. 6717. May 27.

_____. 1971. *Urban design plan for the comprehensive plan of San Francisco.*

_____. 1972. *Chinatown 701 study staff report.*

_____. 1974. *Community safety plan for the comprehensive plan of San Francisco.*

_____. 1978. *Design guidelines for major new developments: An interpretation of the goals & policies of the San Francisco urban design plan.*

_____. 1978. *Final environmental impact report.*

_____. 1979. Annual report 1978-1979.

_____. 1979. *Format & guidelines for preparing an environmental impact report.*

_____. 1979. *Northeastern waterfront survey.*

_____. 1979. *One year interim control.*

_____. 1979. *Summary: Downtown San Francisco conservation & development planning program, phase I study.*

Scott, R.W. 1977. Land use & growth management: A comment for professionals. *Environmental Comment* September: 4-7.

Seattle Department of Community Development. 1971. Seattle urban design report: Determinants of city form.

Skaff, A.Q. 1978. The San Francisco urban design plan: Goals, implementation, & resulting development in the downtown. Unpublished M.C.P. thesis. Berkeley: University of California.

Skidmore, Owings, & Merrill. 1972. *San Antonio urban design mechanism study.* San Antonio: Community Renewal Program, San Antonio City Planning Department.

Skyways help in revival of Minneapolis. 1976. *Houston Post* June 6: A-19.

Smith, S.M. 1976. *Design controls in the urban renewal areas of Salem, Masssachusetts.* Boston, MA: Society for Preservation of New England Antiquities.

Special district zoning for new buildings on Fifth Avenue. 1979. *Progressive Architecture* 60(7): 25-26.

Stephens, S. 1975. Microcosms of urbanity. *Progressive Architecture* 56 (12): 37-38.

Trzyna, T.C. & Jokela, A.W. 1974. *The California environmental quality act; an innovation in state & local decisionmaking.* Los Angeles: Center for California Public Affairs.

Tulane/New Orleans/urban design students view Carrollton plans. 1972. *New Orleans Times-Picayune* May 6: 4-29.

Tucson Department of Planning (n.d.). *Tucson urban design.*

2 U.S. agencies hear opponents to New Orleans Jackson Square plan. 1973. *New Orleans Times-Picayune* November 15: 1-11.

Ugliness of Chicago buildings TV antennas cited. 1976. *Chicago Tribune* March 7: 6-3.

Urban design controls for lower Manhattan waterfront. 1974. *Progressive Architecture* 55(1): 74-75.

Urban Design Council of the City of New York. 1971. *A report on the working relationships of architects & the City of New York.*

_____. 1973. *Housing quality: A program for zoning reform.*

Urban Design Group, New York City Department of City Planning. 1978. *42nd Street study.*

Urban Design Section, Department of City Planning, Norfolk, VA. 1968. *1968 City of Norfolk design awards program.*

Urban design task force to study Hollywood commercial core. 1975. *Los Angeles Times* April 20: IV-7.

Urban designer Ronald Lee Fleming speaks in Los Angeles. 1979. *Los Angeles Times* October 15: IV-1.

Urban Planning & Design Committee, Regional/Urban Design

Assistance Team. 1972. *Butte-RUDAT: Summary report on Butte, Montana.* Washington, DC: American Institute of Architects.

U.S. Department of Housing & Urban Development. 1978. *The community development implementation process: A case study of eleven cities.* Atlanta, GA: U.S. Department of Housing & Urban Development.

U.S. Environmental Protection Agency. 1974. *Promoting environmental quality through urban planning & control.* Washington, DC: U.S. Government Printing Office.

Van Slambrouck, P. 1975. Things are looking up at one market plaza. *San Francisco Business* April: 13-14.

Veri, A.R. et al. 1975. *Environmental quality by design: South Florida.* Coral Gables.

Wagner, W.F., Jr. 1977. New urban policy by an urban mayor. *Architectural Record* 161(3): 13.

Wichita-Sedgwick County Metropolitan Area Planning Department. 1970. *Toward a more livable city: An urban beautification plan for Wichita, Kansas.*

Wiedenhoeft, R. 1975. Minneapolis: A closer look. *Urban Land* 34(9): 8-17.

Wilson, L. 1974. Development rights transfer to build new core. *AIA Journal* 61(3): 51-52.

Yudis, A.J. 1975. 121A looms larger with full valuation. *Boston Sunday Globe* March 16: A-49.

Zoning rebuilds the theater. 1970. *Progressive Architecture* 51(12): 76-78.

Zoning study to enhance residential design. 1979. *Progressive Architecture* 60(1): 106.

Design Review

American Institute of Architects Committee on Design. 1974. *Design review board: A handbook for communities.* Washington, DC: American Institute of Architects.

Bacow, A.F. 1975. *Environmental design review in Brookline, or why have design review, anyway?* Cambridge, MA: Department of Urban Studies & Planning, Massachusetts Institute of Technology.

Baker, R.L. 1976. *Design controls for the built environment: Legal issues in design review*. Boston, MA: Society for the Preservation of New England Antiquities.

Boston Redevelopment Authority. 1967. *The design review process & redevelopers' architectural submissions for housing parcels*.

Brookline (MA) Department of Planning. 1975. *Brookline—a guide to environmental design review*.

———. 1977. *Guide to environmental design review: Vol. 1: for new construction; Vol. 2: for commercial facade*.

Comptroller General of the United States. 1977. *Environmental reviews done by communities: Are they needed? Are they adequate?* Washington, DC: U.S. Government Printing Office.

Lindbloom, C.G. 1970. *Environmental design review*. West Trenton, NJ: Chandler-Davis.

Mylroie, G.R. 1976. Community design review procedures. *Practicing Planner* 6(2): 25-29.

Nally, T. 1977. Design review, alternative models of administration in Boston. Unpublished M.Arch./M.C.P. thesis. Cambridge, MA: Massachusetts Institute of Technology.

Ray, G. 1978. Review of major projects. *Urban Design* 9(1): 14-19.

San Francisco Department of City Planning. 1979. *Environmental review process summary*.

Santa Barbara (CA) Department of Community Development. 1979. *Design review manual*.

Urban Renewal Administration. 1965. *Design review in urban renewal*. Technical guide No. 15. Washington, DC: URA February.

Will, P.S. 1966. Design review in urban renewal: A case study of the Boston Redevelopment Authority. Unpublished M.C.P. thesis. Cambridge, MA: Massachusetts Institute of Technology.

Citizen Participation

Advocacy planning: What it is, how it works. *Progressive Architecture* 49 (9): 102-115.

Appleyard, D. 1979. Community participation in neighborhood design. *Landscape Architecture* 69(5): 487.

Educating citizens to town's industrial history. 1972. *Progressive Architecture* 53(11): 82-85.

Ferebee, A. 1972. Downtown renewal with citizen participation. *Design & Environment* 3(4): 40-47.

Firm aids community participation in housing. 1974. *Design & Environment* 5(2): 40-45.

Kuenne, D.S. 1977. *Sample HUD single purpose small cities program community development block grant citizen participation plan.* Georgetown: Cooperative Extension Service, University of Delaware.

Lewis, D. 1979. Citizen participation in design & planning. *Journal of Architectural Education* 33(1): 27-29.

Lewis, D. & Gindroz, R.L. 1974. Toward design process that re-enfranchizes citizens & consumers. *AIA Journal* 62(5): 28-31.

McClendon, B.W. 1977. Citizen participation in planning: The 'goals for Corpus Christi' experience. *Environmental Comment* November: 8-10.

Miner, D.D. 1977. Citizen involvement: Problems, progress & promise. *Environmental Comment* November: 11-12.

Model cities suit re-establishes citizen participation basis. 1970. *Progressive Architecture* 51(9): 31.

Urban renewal, citizen participation in Shaw Area renewal. 1967. *Architectural Forum* 127(4): 72-77.

Urban renewal: Complexities of citizen participation. 1968. *Architectural Forum* 128(4): 58-63.

Workbook to aid citizen decisions on preservation & growth. 1978. *Progressive Architecture* 59(1): 92-93.